Bead Crochet Euro

Ann Benson

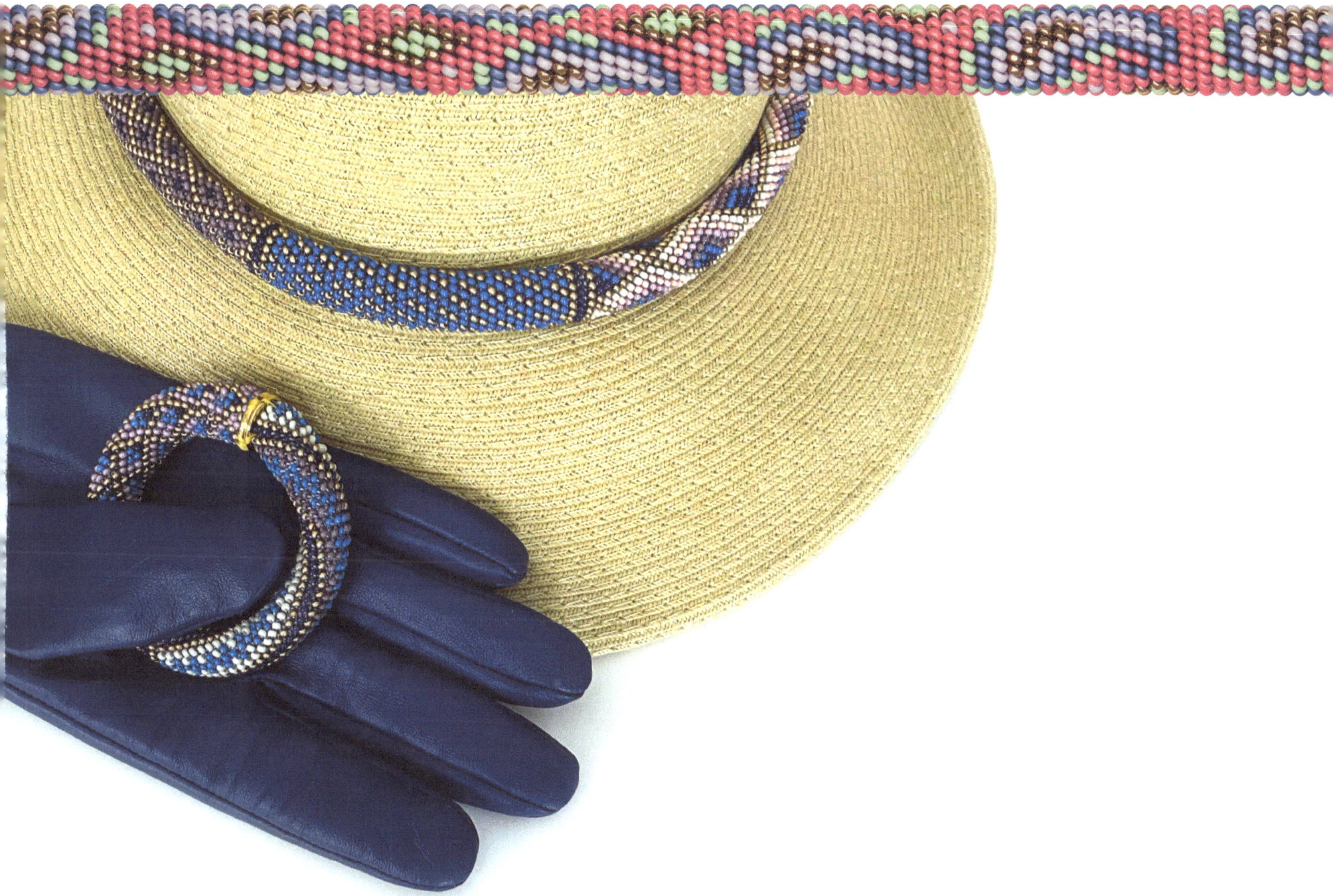

for Mary-Christine
ma chère amie

1

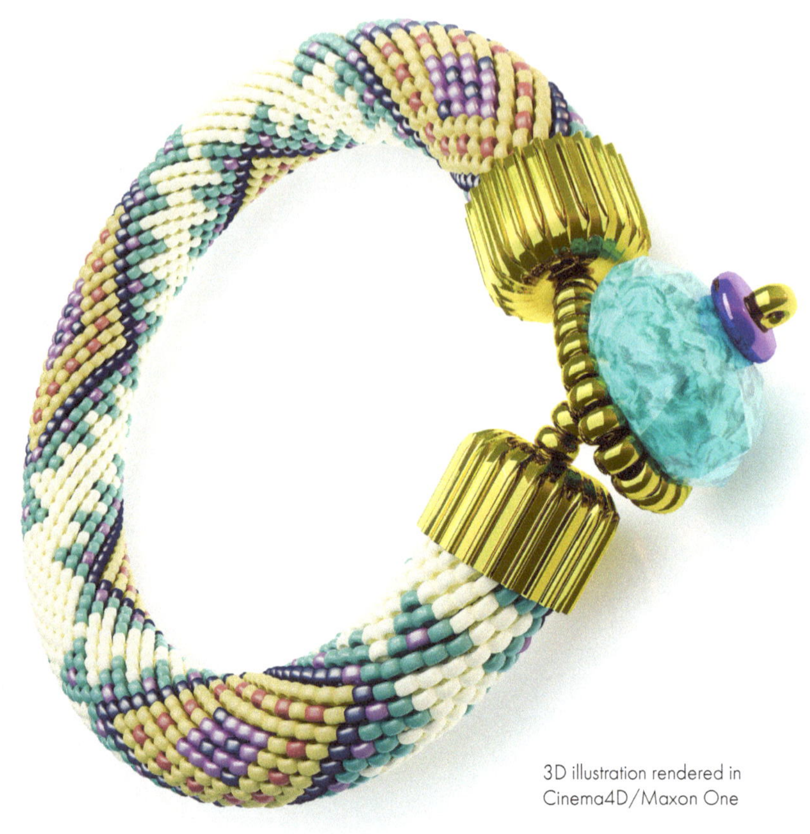

3D illustration rendered in
Cinema4D/Maxon One

ann benson
beading

Cover photo ©2024 Gary Frost, used with permission
Design assistance by Ella Farland

Many thanks to Prof. Dina Zaccagnini Vincent, Rhode Island
School of Design, for excellent critique and wise advice, and to
my classmates in Graphic Design for their gentle support.

Euro

Not your average crocheted tube.

The name Euro comes from its origin in eastern Europe, where its modern version is popular and widely practiced. It's also called Double bead crochet—a misnomer, as there are no double crochet stitches—and Harness bead crochet, a translation error, as there is nary a harness in sight.

The technique you're likely most familiar with is tubular bead crochet, which encloses a bead within a spiral of slip stitch, with the bead positioned near the end of the stitch process. Slip stitch tubes are fairly stiff and (depending on your personal stitch tension) can be somewhat resistant to bending. Euro bead crochet uses a single crochet stitch with the bead slipped at the start of the stitch process. Tubes worked in Euro are softer and more flexible and can have dozens of stitches in the circumference.

Both techniques have the same goal: to put the bead on the outside of a spiral of thread crochet.

I have the goal of getting you to a place where you can enjoy either technique with a modicum of agility and grace. Let's get started.

COMPANION VIDEO ON ANN BENSON'S YOUTUBE CHANNEL:

https://youtu.be/b27oiGcC1uU

Contents

eurobeadcrochet.annbenson

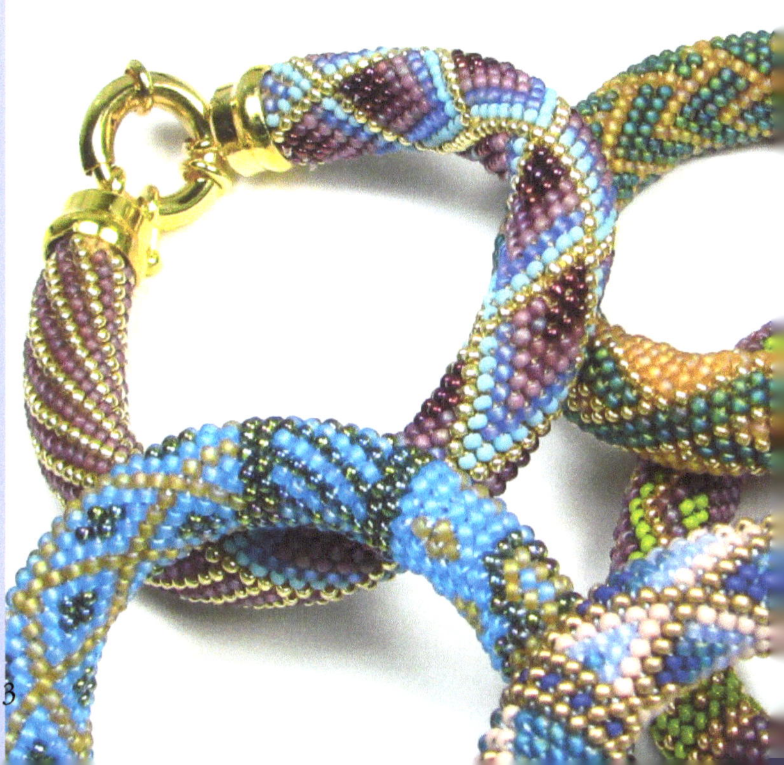

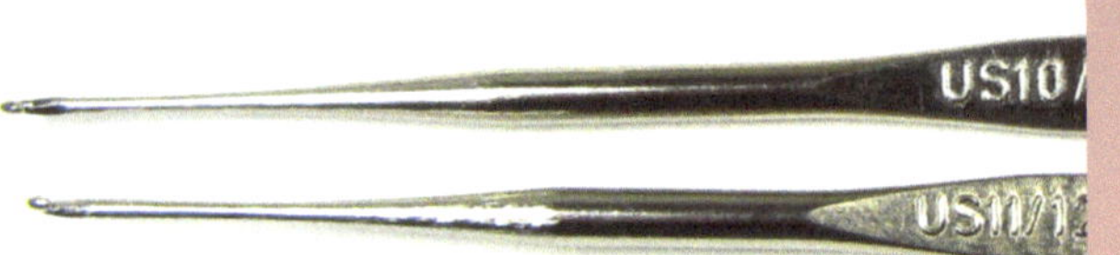

Putting materials and tools together for a perfect result

The queen bee of this hive is always the bead.

Beads are rigid in size and shape—the hook, threading needle, and crochet thread must all bow to her demands. Size 11° is most frequently used in this technique (widely available!), but 8°s and Japanese 15°s (Preciosa 15°s are too small) can also be used. After a couple of projects you can brave up and experiment with other sizes and shapes!

Material wisdoms

Thread must be strong and stable—it should not break or stretch when snapped. Co-ordinate thread color to the dominant bead color.

Do not use cheap threading needles. They're stamped and then polished, so don't skimp. You'll regret the un-smooth experience.

Your hook should feel comfortable in your hand. Some brands have padded handles or ergonomic shapes. These are a worthwhile investment in hand health.

Good quality beads will be the most consistent in size and shape. Reject beads that are misshapen or rough.

Certain bead finishes are unstable and should not be used, most notably dyed or galvanized beads with a "painted" on metallic finish. These are found in vintage beads but are not produced in the same manner now by the major providers (Miyuki, Toho, Preciosa, Matsuno). Now coatings are often "baked" on through a stable process that is far more resistant to wear and cosmetics. The safest "colors" are color-through (fused into the glass) with simple coatings like matte, lustered, Ceylon, and aurora borealis (AB).

11°s — **HOOK** steel size 9 (1.25mm) or steel size 10 (1.15mm)

THREADING NEEDLE size 10 embroidery, size 9 or 10 darner

CROCHET THREAD size 12 or 16 perle cotton, Cebelia 20 or 30

8°s — **HOOK** steel size 9 (1.25mm) or steel size 8 (1.35mm)

THREADING NEEDLE size 9 embroidery, size 9 darner

CROCHET THREAD size 10 or 8 perle cotton

15°s — **HOOK** steel size 11/12 (1mm) or steel size 13/14 (.9mm)

THREADING NEEDLE size 12 embroidery, size 12 beading

CROCHET THREAD size 16 perle cotton, size 20/2 mercerized cotton, heavy duty mercerized sewing thread

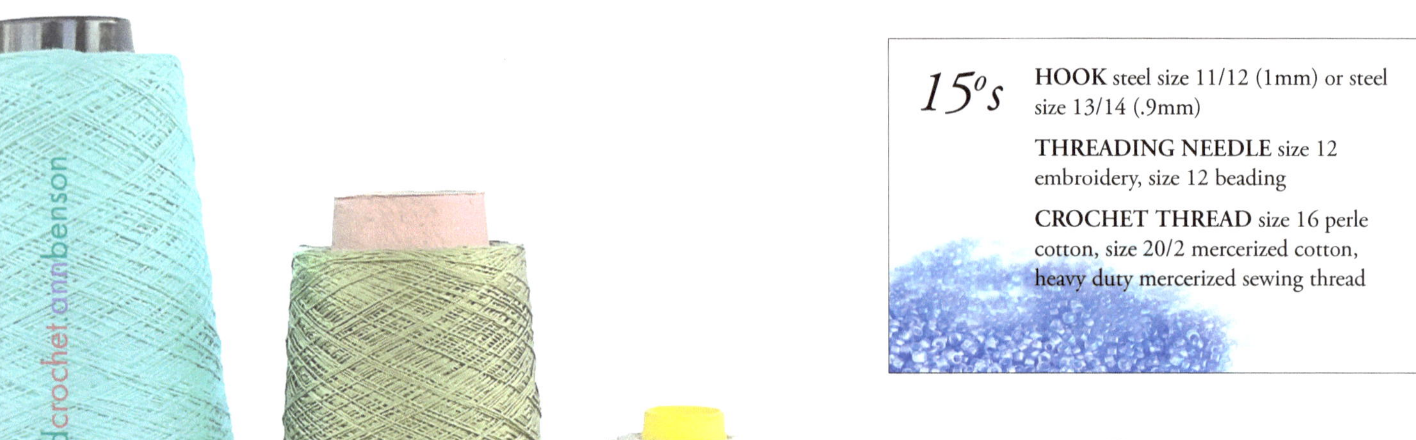

4

Figuring materials

Where bead quantities are given with charts or patterns, it shows the number of beads required for **ONE INCH OF CROCHETED TUBE.** In this example the circumference is 15 beaded stitches. The pattern repeat has sixty-four (64) beads in two colors, rust and cream. You want to make a 7" tube for a bracelet using predominantly Japanese 11° seed beads on perle cotton thread.

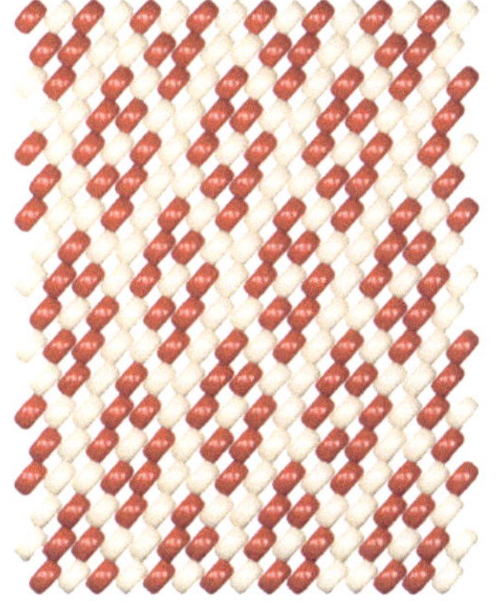

PATTERN SINGLE REPEAT

There are roughly **13/14 (9/10) (17/18) rounds** of crochet per inch of tube length using 11° (8°) (Japanese 15°) seed beads.

Seed beads are sold in grams; **one gram of 11° (8°) (Japanese 15°) has 90/100 (40-45) (275) beads per gram.**

Using 11° (8°) 15°) beads, **each stitch on size 12 or 16 perle cotton requires .75" (.9") (.6") of thread.**

Threads are sold by gram ball, cone or wound spool. **One gram size 12 perle cotton has about 14 yards/13 meters, size 16 about 15.5 yards/14 meters.** Check with manufacturers for other types of thread.

PATTERN CHART

To determine the number of beads per pattern and the number of each color bead within the pattern, the best method is the oldest one: simply **count them from the diagram** if that information is not given.

Using the counted numbers, **the formula below shows how to figure the needed amounts** for this project; by plugging in the number for your own project you can figure those amounts easily.

BEAD BRAND CODES

PR = Preciosa (Czech)

MI = Miyuki (Japanese)

TO = Toho (Japanese)

MA = Matsuno (Japanese)

1 Figure the number of beaded stitches.
Fourteen rounds per inch x 8 inches = 112 rounds
112 rounds x 15 circumference = 1680 beaded stitches

2 Figure the number of pattern repeats
1680 beads /64 beads per pattern = 26.25, round up to 27

3 Count the number of each bead color per pattern
Rust beads per pattern = 32 x 27 = 864 rust beads needed
Cream beads per pattern = 32 x 27 = 864 cream beads needed
864 beads/90 beads per gram = 9.6 grams of each color

4 Figure the amount of thread length needed
1680 x .75" per stitch = 1260" (3200 cm) = 35 yards/32 meters

Euro crochet (in keeping with ALL forms of bead crochet) is an **exercise in thread management.** Keeping your thread contained and healthy is simpler than you might think with a bit of preparation.

Pair your thread, needle and beads as we've previously described.

Prepare the end of your thread as shown in this photo. First wet the end of the thread, then flatten it between your fingertips. **Trim the thread end clean** at a diagonal angle.

Examine the eye of your needle. Needles are stamped out of metal and then polished; the side where the stamp enters the metal blank will have a wider hole.

WET THE EYE OF THE NEEDLE so the moisture draws in the thread. Push the trimmed wet thread through the eye and draw it through. You can use a tweezer to facilitate this.

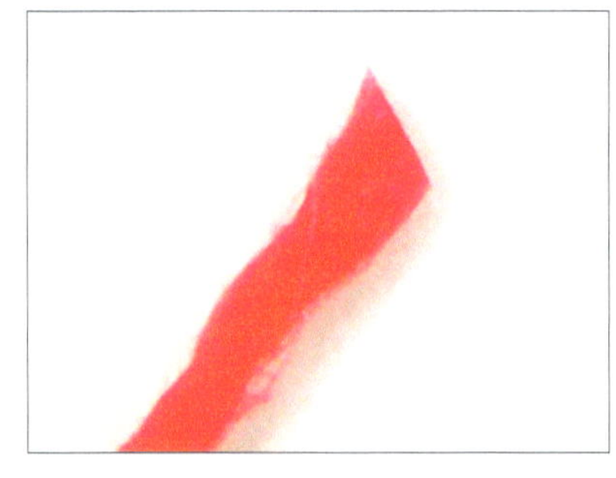

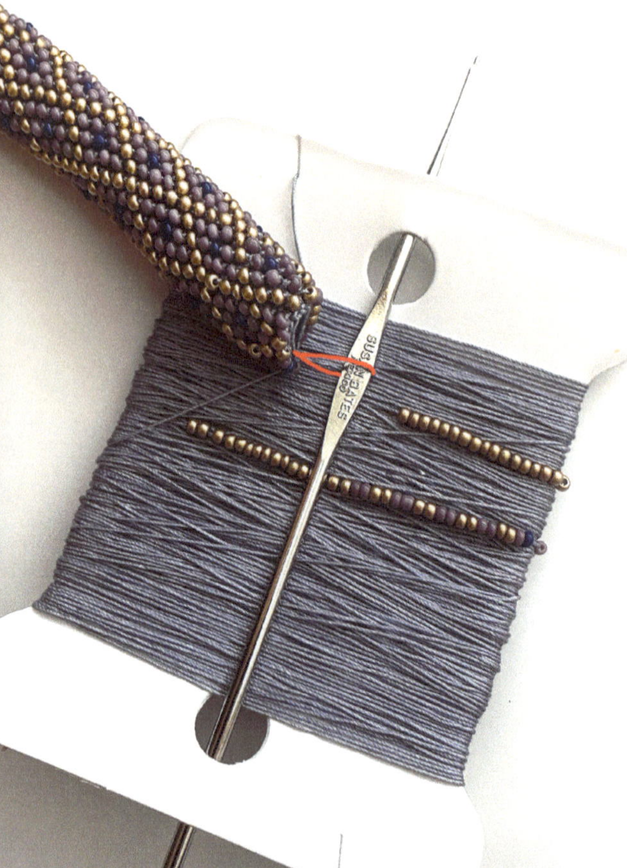

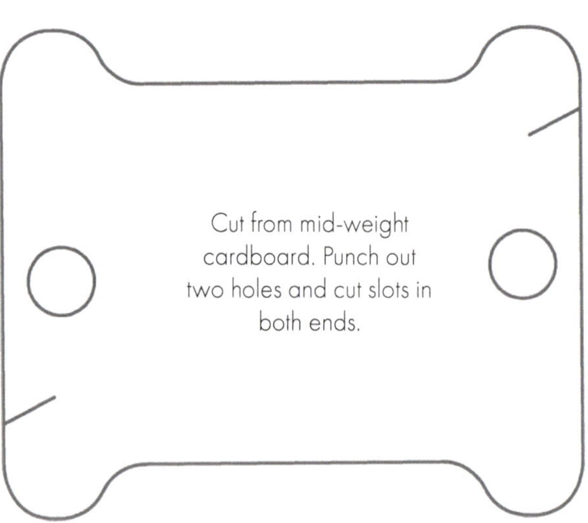

Cut from mid-weight cardboard. Punch out two holes and cut slots in both ends.

Wind your thread directly onto the card before loading the beads. Load the beads, pull out some slack, and wrap the beaded thread around the card. Crochet your design, pulling out thread and bringing beads down the thread as needed. When it's time to put your crochet away, wrap the uncrocheted thread around the card. Keep your hook in the working loop (shown **RED**) and stick the two ends of the hook through the holes in the winding card. This keeps both your thread and your working loop secure.

Getting the beads onto the thread

Because we read left to right, the charted and horizontal patterns herein are shown threaded left to right. It's important to remember that the last bead threaded is the first bead crocheted.

Threading short linear patterns

When the number of beads in a repeating pattern is less than the number of beads in the round, simply **thread patterns presented horizontally from LEFT TO RIGHT**, adding as many repeats as you think you will need for the desired length. Short patterns can often be memorized. For ease of threading, you can lay out your beads in small piles in the order of threading then pick up one bead from each pile in order.

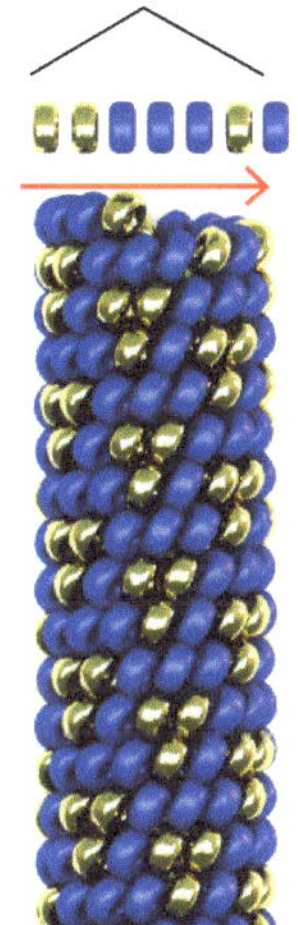

ONE REPEAT

The beads in the first pile on the left can be counted prior to threading; add the number of beads in this pile to match the number of pattern repeats in your design. If you reject a bead, be sure to add another. In this manner, you won't have to keep track of how many repeats you have threaded.

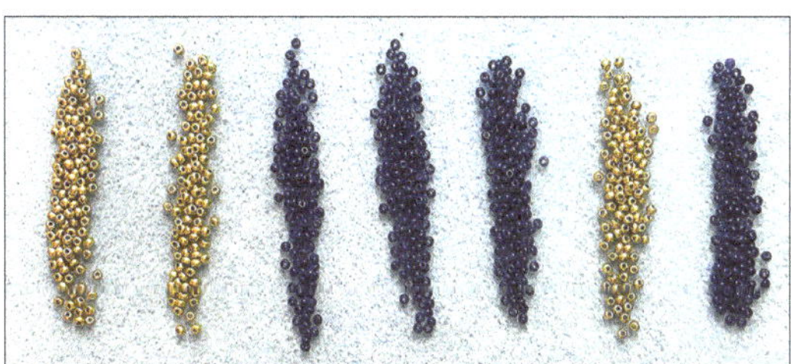

BEADS LAID OUT IN PATTERN IN SMALL PILES

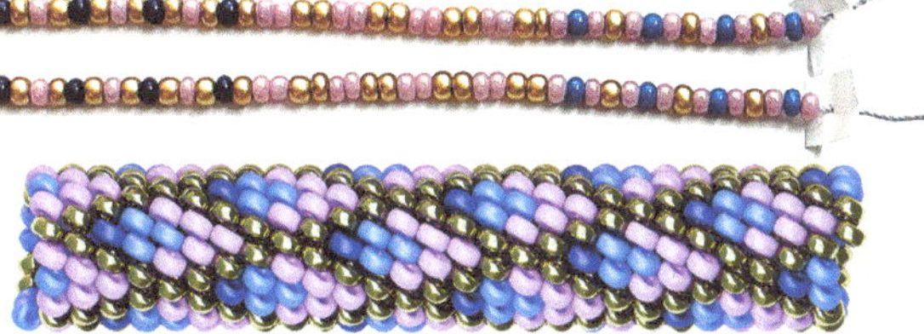

Using paper markers

Use paper markers at the end of the pattern repeat; one pattern repeat is used as the template for all subsequent repeats after being carefully checked for accuracy.

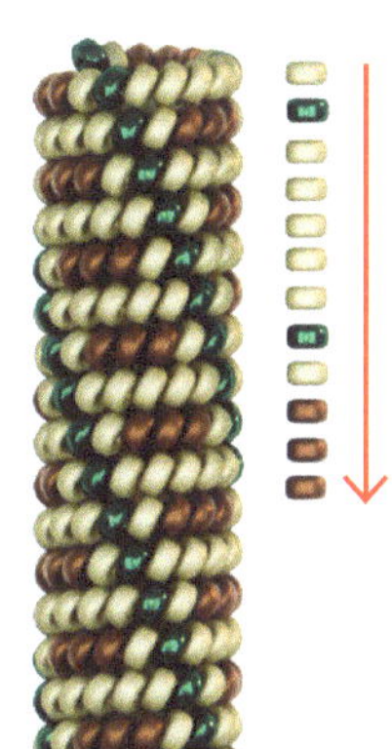

If a simple pattern is presented **vertically thread it from TOP TO BOTTOM**, again adding the required number of repeats.

You can keep track of repeats in simple patterns by noting an easily-recognized motif within the pattern. For example, in this pattern you could count the number of groups of three dark copper beads.

Threading longer linear patterns

Some patterns for Euro crochet have dozens of beads in one repeat. In many cases these patterns can still be presented in a linear fashion, which is ultimately easier to read.

You can keep track of the number of repeats you've threaded by placing a paper marker on the thread at the end of each repeat and then counting the markers.

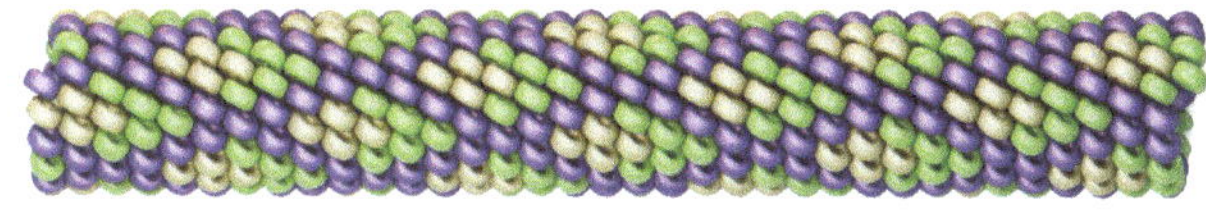

Sometimes a repeating pattern that is presented as a flat chart can be used as a linear pattern; the starting and ending beads of each repeat will be highlighted

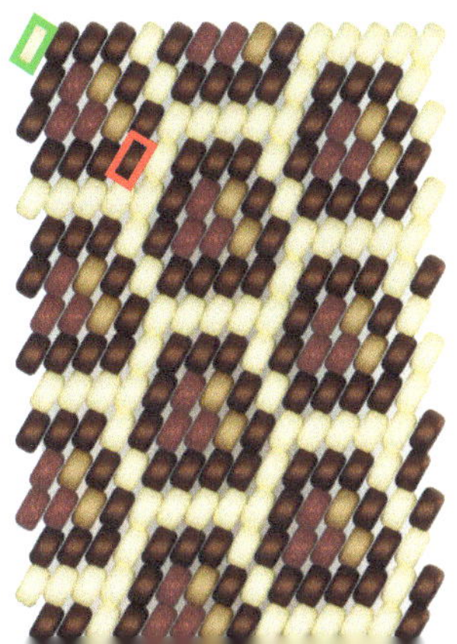

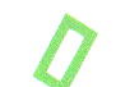
FIRST BEAD OF ONE PATTERN REPEAT

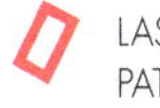
LAST BEAD OF ONE PATTERN REPEAT

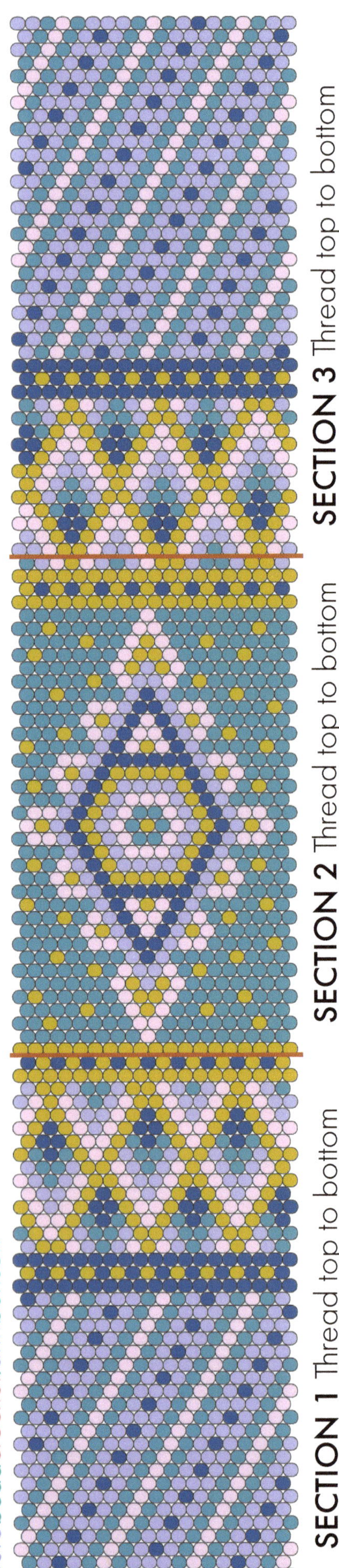

Threading from a charted pattern

We read left to right but most right-handed stitchers crochet right to left. Because **90% of us are right-handed**, the crocheted tube will develop in mirror image/upside-down to a charted design. For left-handed crocheters, the pattern will not be mirrored.

Because beads are heavy and thread can tangle (a disaster) it's wise to thread most bracelet-length or longer projects in sections. Again, remember that the last bead threaded will be the first bead crocheted so **the bottom section should be threaded first, the middle section next, and the top section last.** You're still threading left to right, top to bottom.

Use a piece of paper positioned directly under the line you're threading. Move the paper down the chart as you progress. Often I will use masking tape which is easily removed and replaced to secure the paper in place. Another good thing to consider is to scan and print out the pattern, then dot or cross out lines as you progress. You're preserving your original pattern and making your threading an easier prospect.

Thread beads by solid rows, left to right, top row to bottom row.

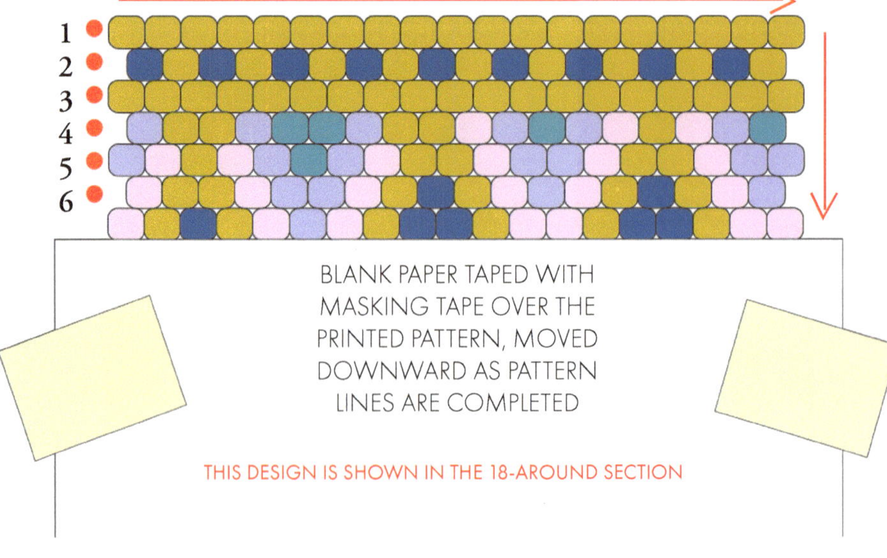

More complex designs may be shown in expanded rows for ease of reading. These are also threaded top row to bottom row, left to right.

The beads are threaded. Now what?

Every spiral tube starts with a foundation of chain stitches with one more stitches than your design has in each round.

Every chain starts with a slip knot. Pull out a foot of thread, form a "pretzel" shape, placing threads over and under as shown here. Insert the hook.

Pull up the hook to form a loop. Adjust the thread as needed, leaving a tail of 10" (25.4 cm). It helps to grasp the knot as you draw the loop up and in.

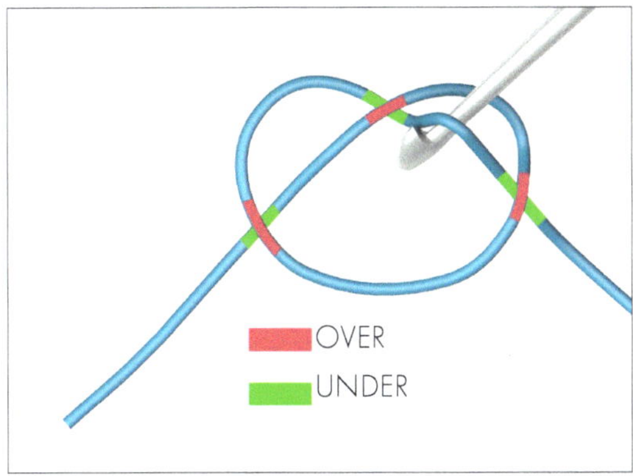

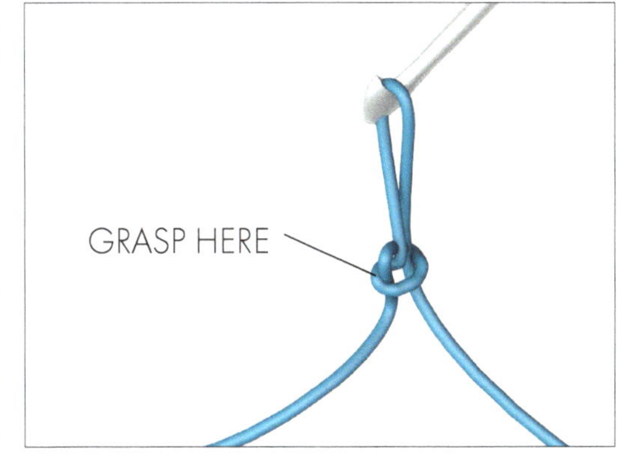

Wrap the thread around the hook. Here the thread is shown wrapped front to back, but back to front works just as well. Keep the slip knot fairly loose as you'll be using it again.

Pull the wrapped thread through the slip knot loop to form the first chain.

Finish the stitch by adjusting it to create a neat loop. Use this stitch as a model for the size of all subsequent chains.

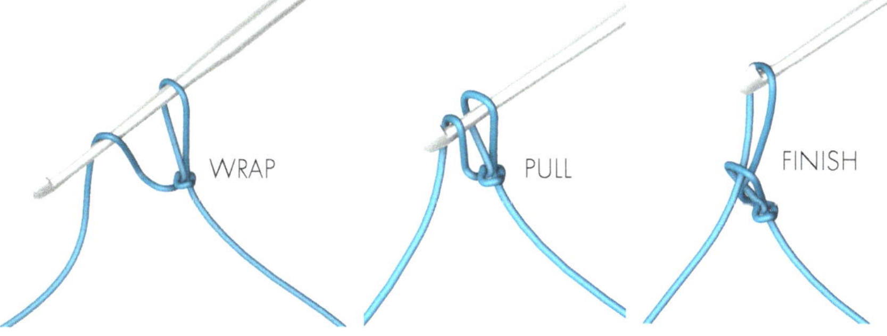

Repeat these actions until you have the desired number of chain stitches. Keep the chains as even as possible, and watch your tension—it's difficult to insert the hook into a chain stitch that's overly tight.

Each chain will subsequently be the foundation for a single crochet stitch, either with or without a bead.

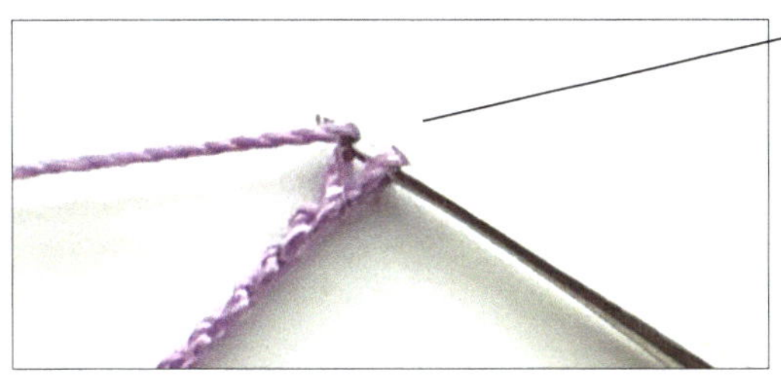

The best method for keeping your stitches even and consistent is to pay attention to the size of this loop before pulling the thread through it. Adjust each chain to achieve the same rough size of this loop.

WORKING THREAD

This is the first single crochet stitch of the round (details, next page)

TAIL THREAD which will later be secured within the crochet

The devil is always in the details.

Working in the whole stitch

In the diagram at right, you can see the three parts of the crochet stitch loop: the back of the loop, the whole loop and the front of the loop. You should **ALWAYS insert the hook through the whole loop.**

That said, in the first few rounds **it can be a challenge to insert the hook through the whole loop** as the stitches will turn inward until the tube has seven or eight rounds completed. It's not the end of the world if you do a few back loops when you simply can't get the hook through the whole loop.

Once the tube is established, however, beads in stitches that are not made through the whole loop will be looser and may protrude a bit from the rest of the tube.

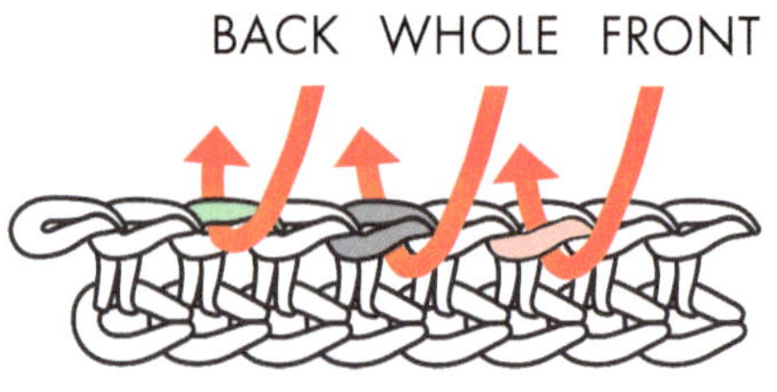

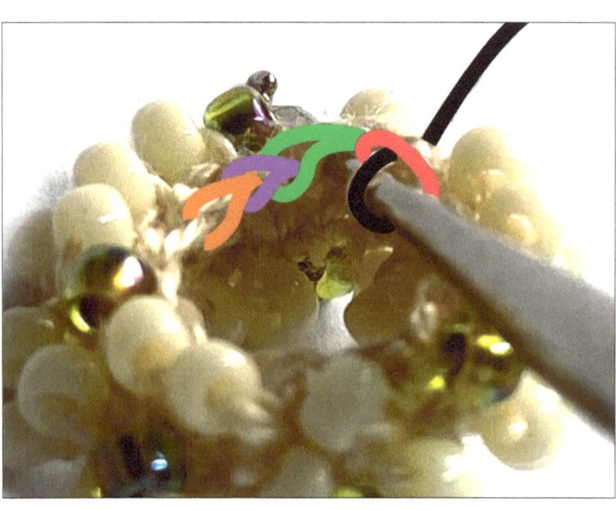

Identifying the loops

In this diagram the whole loops and working thread and loop of the round in the early start of a tube are shown clearly. **In the first few rounds you'll need to make a specific effort to use the whole loop.**

- Working loop and thread
- Last stitch made
- Loop through which you insert the hook
- Next whole stitch loop
- Another whole stitch loop

Keeping the bead on the outside of the stitch

The whole point of creating a tube of beads is to have the **beads on the outside and the fiber stitches on the inside.** In photo A, the thread is wrapped from back to front over the hook prior to pulling it through. In photo B, **the thread is grabbed from behind and under, which is the preferred manner,** as the bead naturally falls to the outside.

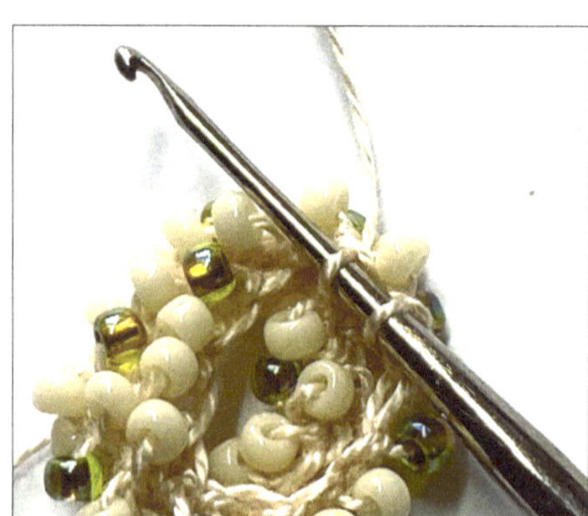

In this photo, you can see the bead on the outside prior to pulling the thread through the two loops on the hook

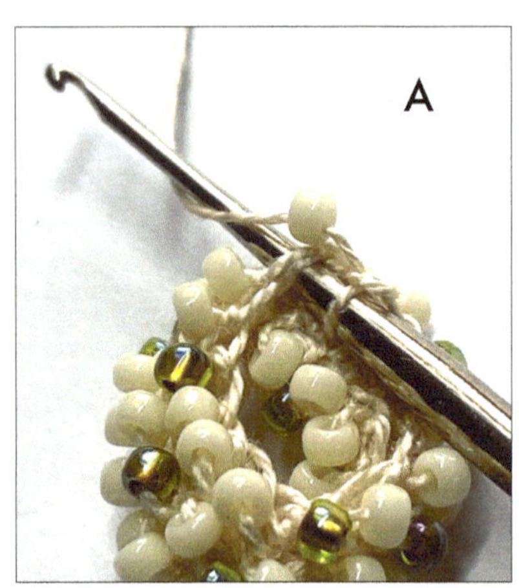

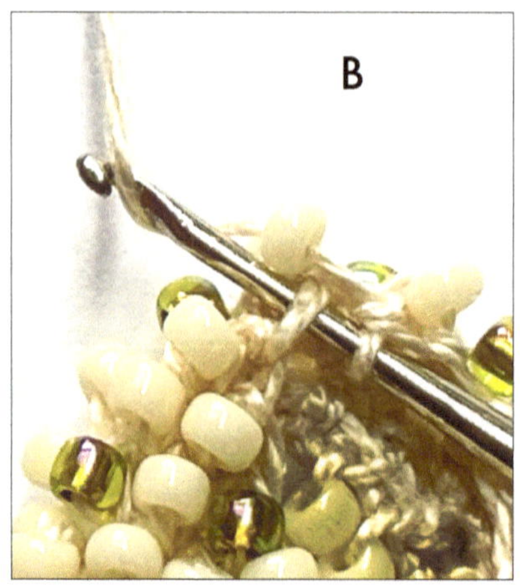

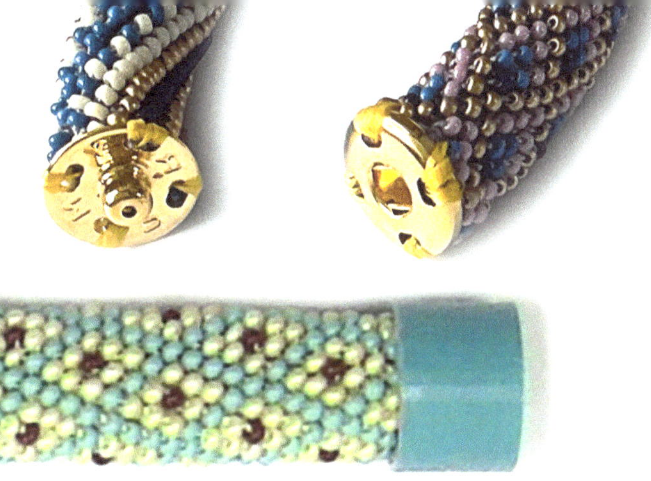

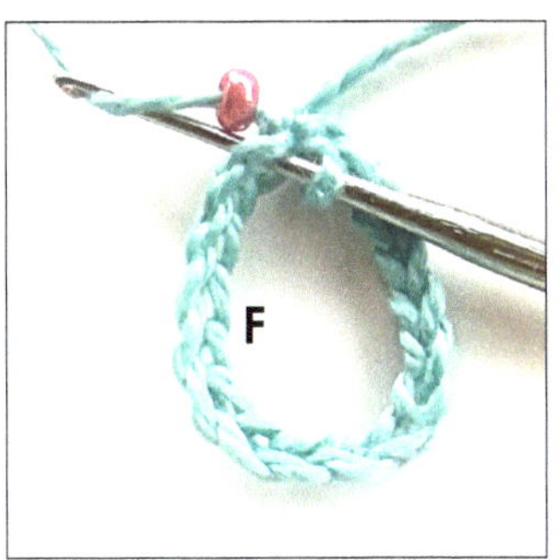

If you want to insert the entire end of the tube into a closure or use a snap, start your beaded crochet directly on the foundation chain.

Insert the hook into the first chain and bring a bead down the working thread; wrap the thread round the hook. (F). **Pull the thread** through the chain (G) which catches the bead on the outside of the chain. **Wrap the thread** around the hook (H) and **pull the wrapped thread** through both loops on the hook (I).

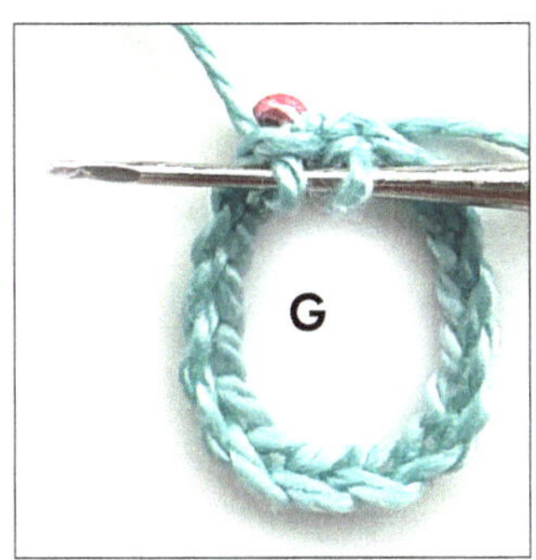

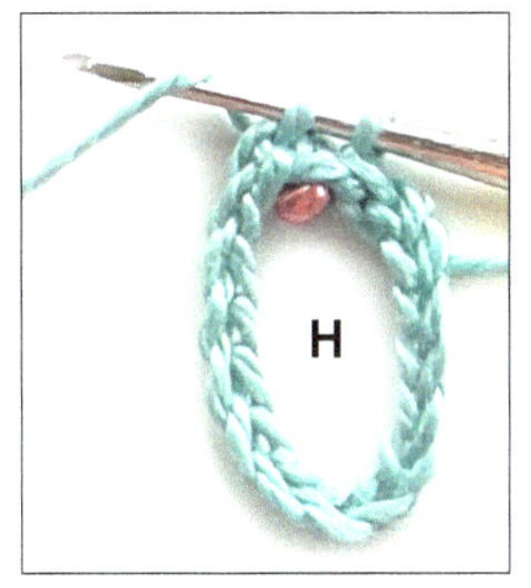

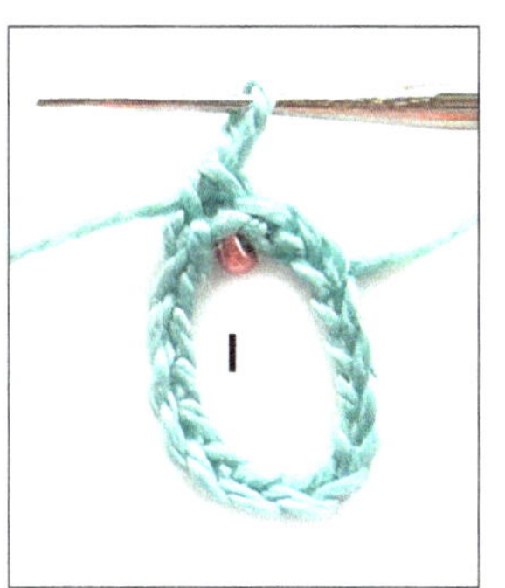

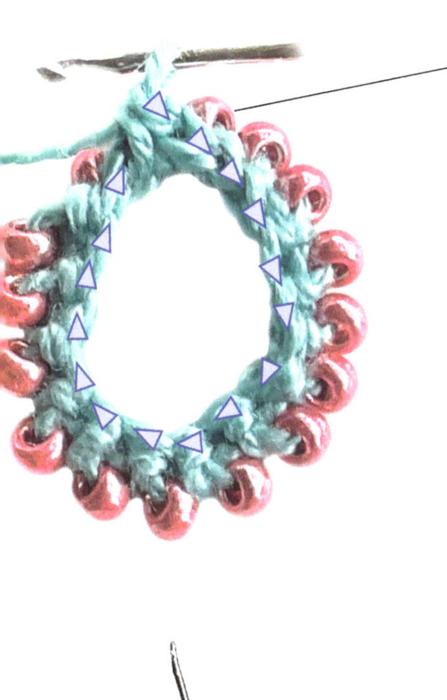

All sixteen beaded stitches are shown here, though the last bead added is hiding behind the working loop.

The red and blue dots (below, right) show how **the tube is beginning to form a spiral.** As the beaded crochet progresses, the spiral will be better defined.

The first bead will not initially land in the same position as it will when more rounds are added. Here it looks to be on the inside of the chain, but in reality it is on the outside and will be more visibly so with the addition of beaded rounds. The beads will shift slightly clockwise as rounds are added.

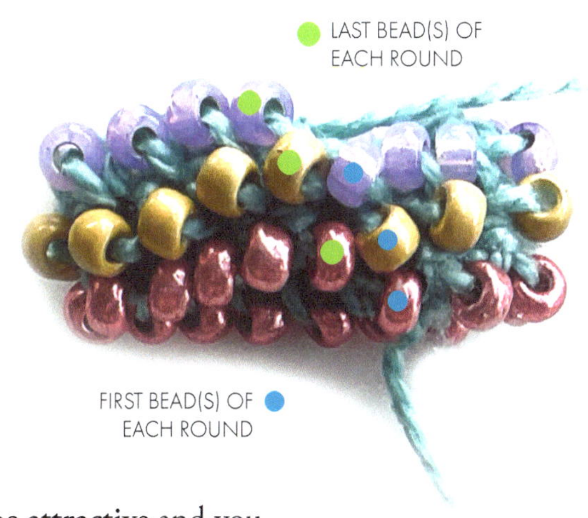

The first ten or so rounds will not be attractive and you may be tempted to start over or quit altogether. But after a few more rounds, the tube will take form and will be easier to handle.

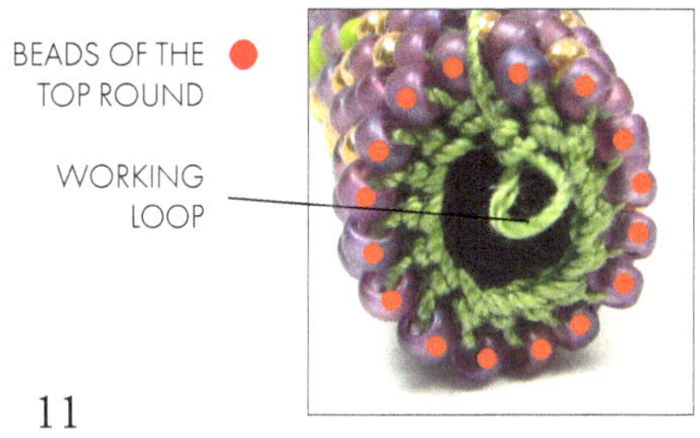

If you want the edge of your beaded tube to be flush with the edge of the clasp, work a few rounds of spiral single crochet *without* beads so the crochet fits inside the clasp.

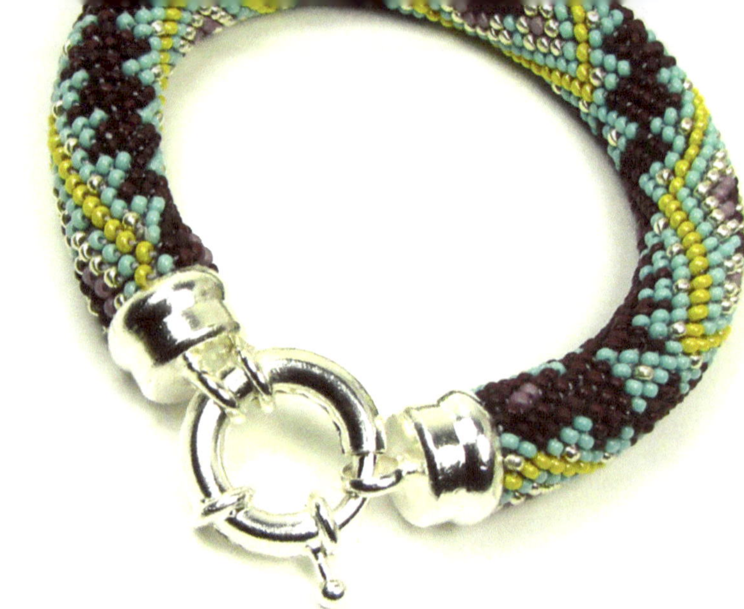

To get the spiral started, **use the first chain you made** as the basis for the first single crochet stitch. There is no "step-up" as there is in traditional single crochet.

Insert the hook into the chain (A). **Wrap the working thread** around the hook (B) and **pull it through** (C). **Wrap the working thread** around the hook (D) and **pull it through** to form the first single crochet (E). Thereafter, make a single crochet stitch in each chain. Continue without stepping up to form a spiral.

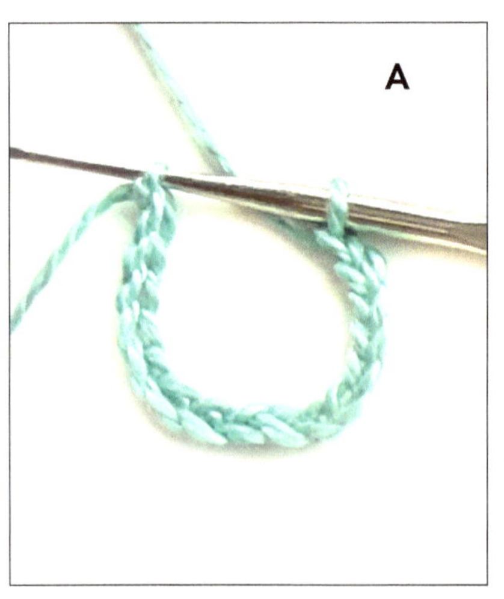

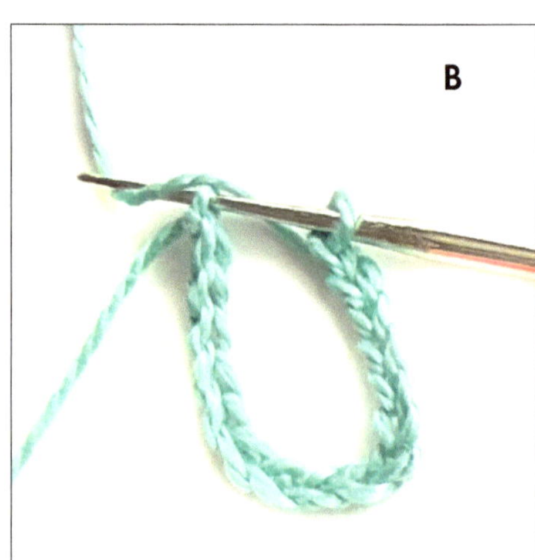

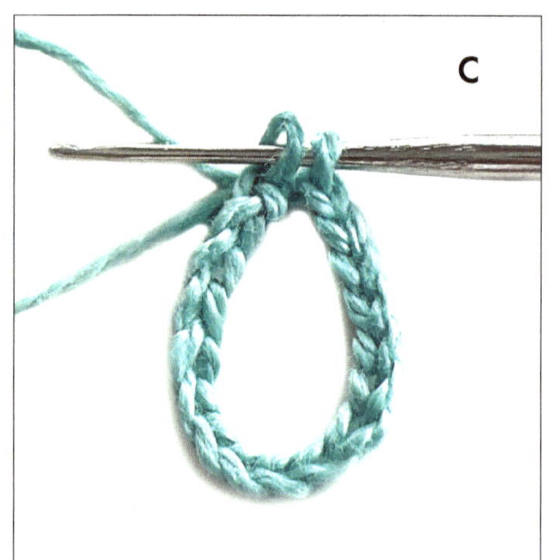

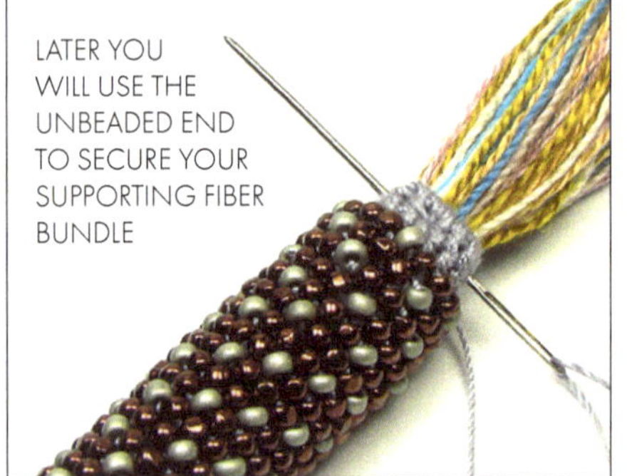

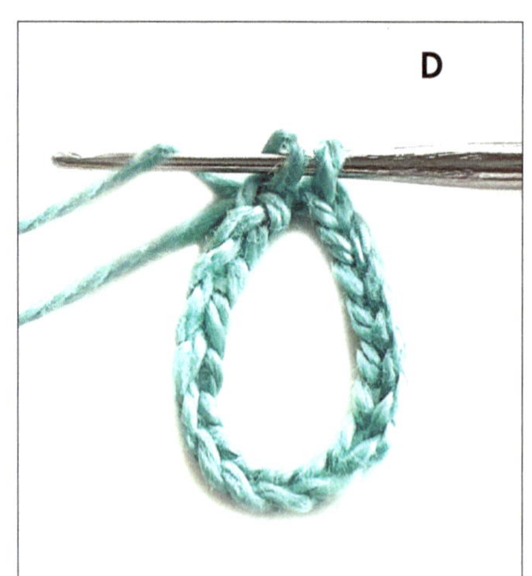

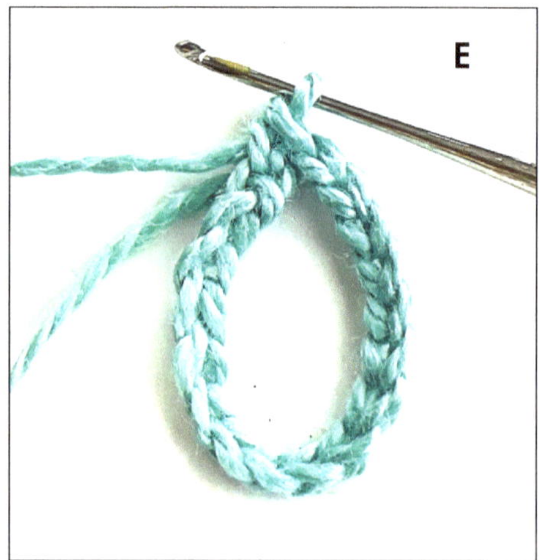

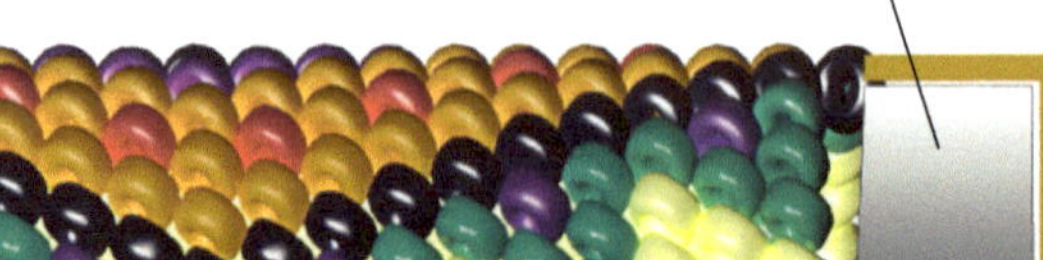

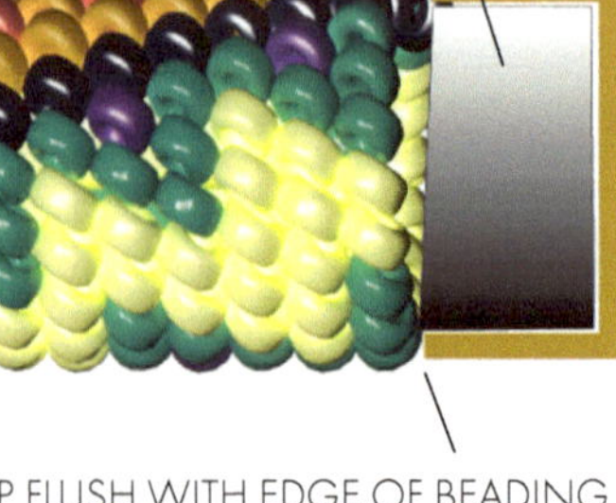

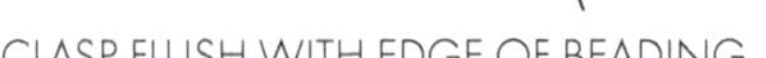

CLASP FLUSH WITH EDGE OF BEADING

An essential skill if you thread your beads in sections or if you're correcting a threading error

Your hook is in the working loop of the last stitch of the joining point. You've cut your thread leaving a six inch tail. The beads of the section you're joining are completely threaded.

Pull the new thread (red) through the last loop of the first section to create a new working loop. Tighten the old thread. Use (optional) masking tape to secure the loose thread ends to the side of the tube.

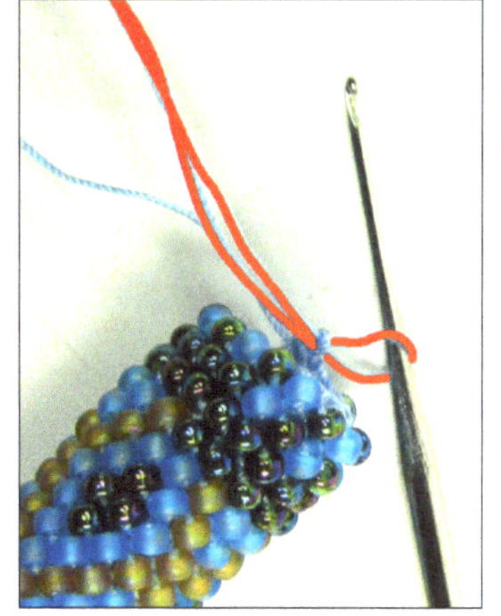
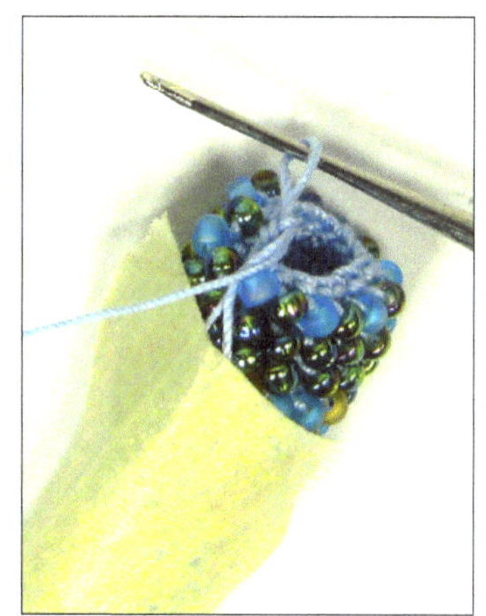

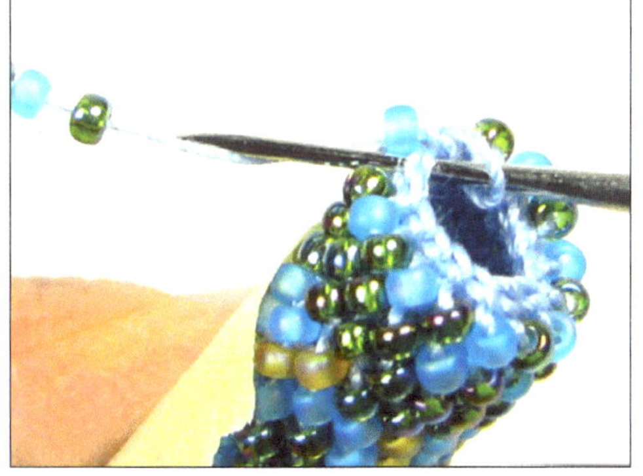

Bring a bead down the new thread and insert the hook in the next stitch; finish the stitch as usual with the new thread. Continue crocheting as if the new thread were the old thread. Check that the beads are lining up correctly in pattern.

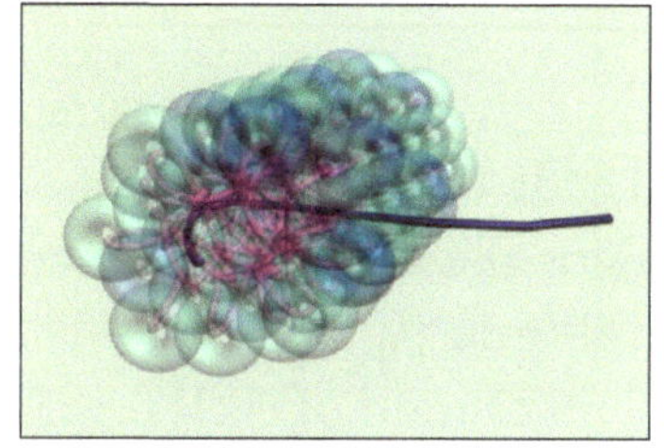

Keep all tails within the fiber wall when burying them; the channel must remain open for finishing

When you have four or five rounds beyond the join point, remove the tape. Secure the thread tails within the fiber walls of the tube, but NOT through the center of the channel, which must remain open for finishing. Take several short invisible stitches with each thread tail, then trim close to the beads, taking care not to cut stitching threads.

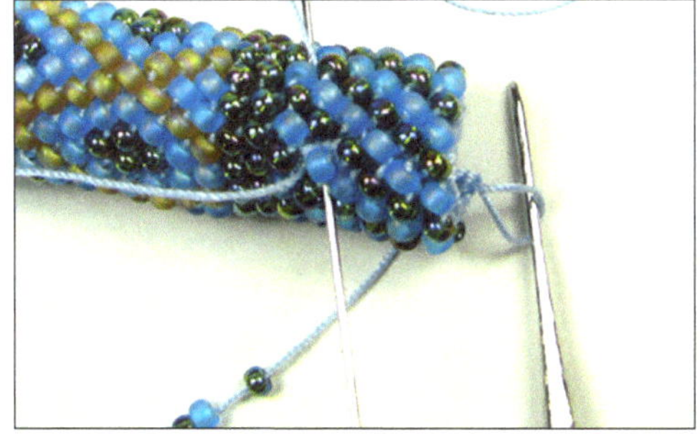
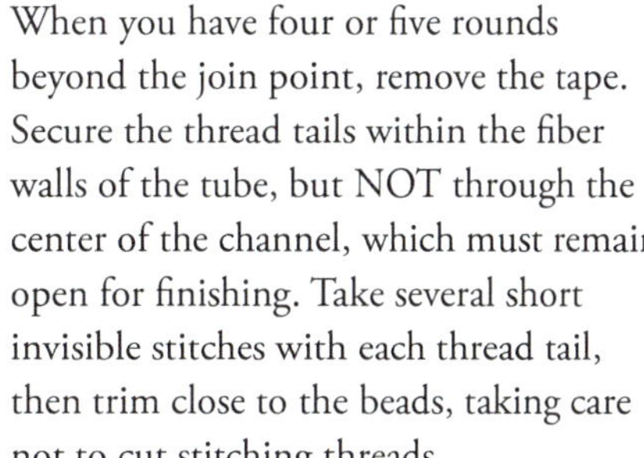

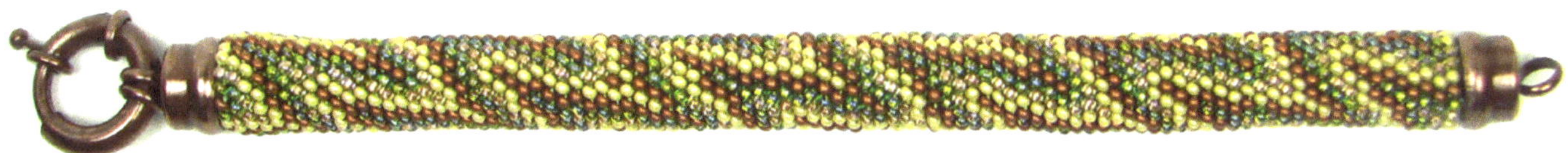

This bracelet was crocheted in four sections, each joined invisibly to the previous section. None of the joints are discernible.

Increasing/decreasing

You can change the circumference of a tube mid-stream.

Increasing the number of beads in each round can be accomplished using **different methods,** entirely up to you.

1 Work two beaded stitches into one beaded stitch. Simply add a second beaded stitch to one whole loop on the top round. The bead is placed immediately, making it easier to count the stitches in the round. This is my preferred method; it yields the most seamless appearance at the increase point, but it is more difficult to insert the hook into the whole loop of the increase stitch.

2 Add a second unbeaded stitch into one stitch. Work the rest of the beaded round, and when you reach the unbeaded stitch, be sure to work a beaded stitch into it.

3 Work a chain stitch at the increase point. In the next round, treat the chain as if it were a whole loop and make a beaded stitch in it. In this method the location of your increase may be more visible.

This subtly shaped tube **starts at 13-around and ends at 20-around.** Dotted pattern sections all have fourteen rows (1" in 11°s) and all are separated by five-round bands. **The first round of each separator band is where the increase takes place.**

To create a design with this type of shaping, thread the widest section first. Separator bands can be solid or slightly patterned; **the increase takes place in the first round** of the separator if there is a pattern, and in the center round of the separator if it is one solid color. Similarly, decreases take place in the last round of the separator.

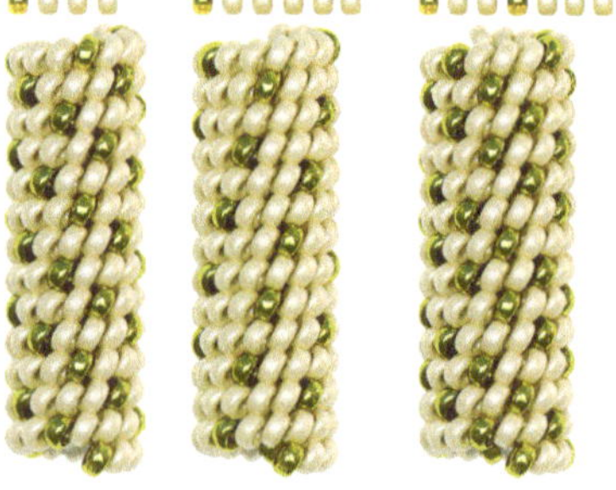

13-around
46 repeats

14-around
33 repeats

15-around
30 repeats

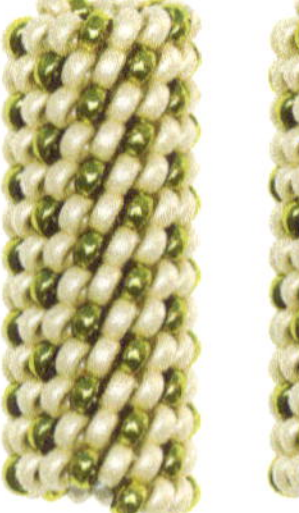

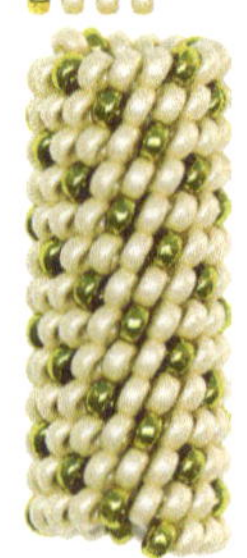

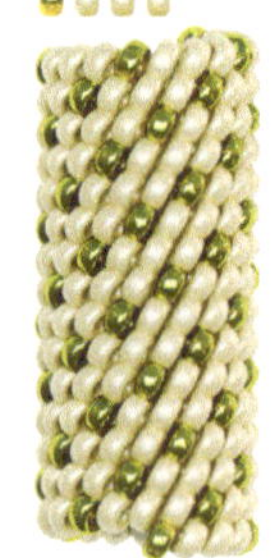

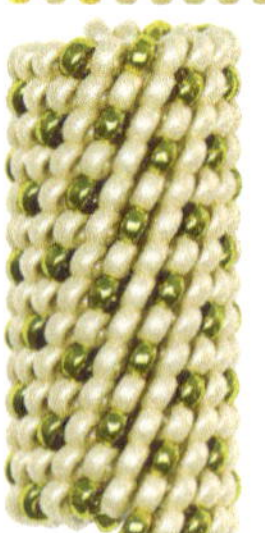

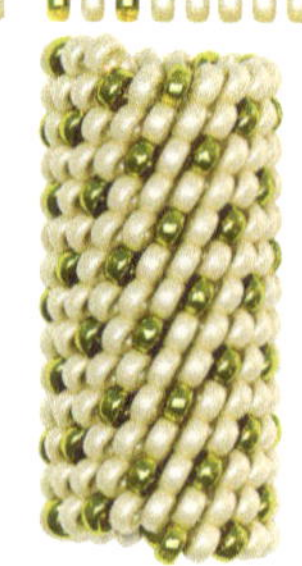

16-around
75 repeats

17-around
60 repeats

18-around
63 repeats

19-around
33 repeats

20-around
35 repeats

Decreasing is more simple. After pulling up the second loop in the whole loop of the stitch at the increase point, insert the hook through the whole loop of the NEXT stitch. Do not bring a bead down the thread. Wrap the thread around the hook and pull through all THREE loops on the hook.

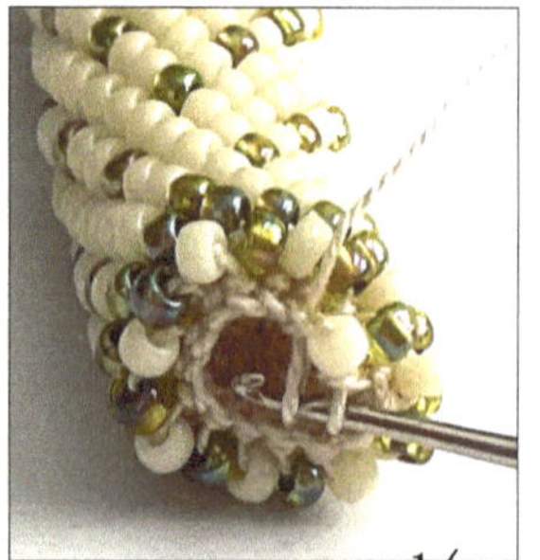

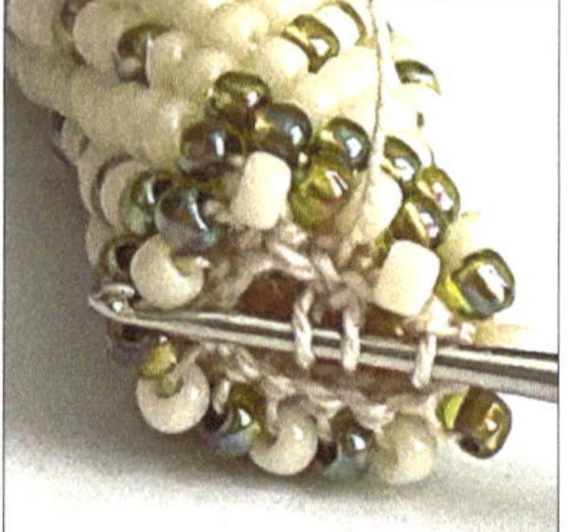

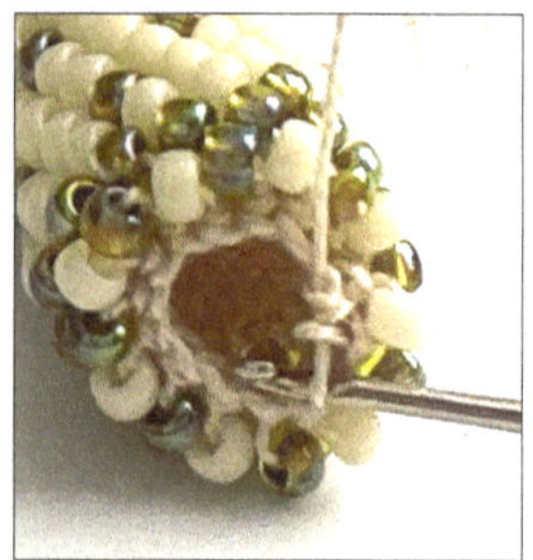

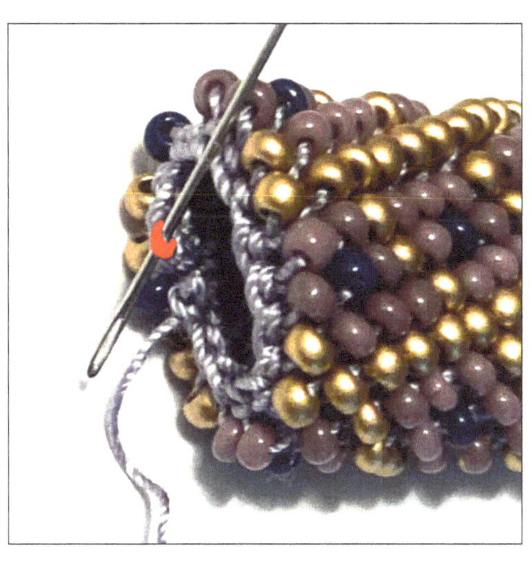

Reclaiming a dropped stitch

Sometimes you just *have to* drop a stitch to complete your day.

The most important element in reclaiming that stitch is to i**dentify the correct loop.** In the photo at left, the working stitch is shown in RED.

Keep a threading needle on hand and run it through the loop. **Pull on the bead of the previous stitch**; if the stitch doesn't ravel out, you've got the right loop.

If you don't test the loop and mistakenly proceed with the incorrect loop, everything you've crocheted before that stitch will pull out with the slightest tug. After crocheting a round or so, check that your pattern is lining up correctly.

Correcting a threading error

It's fairly good news if you have too many beads, less good news if you missed one.

You can break out an extra bead. NEVER BREAK OUT A BEAD WITHOUT WEARING EYE PROTECTION or with anyone nearby not wearing eye protection. Pull out a few stitches and secure the working loop. Place the bead (with the thread) on a sturdy flat surface that you don't care about marring; it may take some juggling to get the bead to lay almost flat. Place the point of your hook on top of the bead hole and press down hard. The bead will break outward. Check your thread to be sure it's sound and then continue crocheting.

If you've skipped a bead in the threading, move the uncrocheted beads down the thread so you have about ten inches of unbeaded thread. Cut the thread at the halfway point. Put a threading needle on the beaded uncrocheted thread and add the required beads. Proceed as if you were joining a new thread for sections.

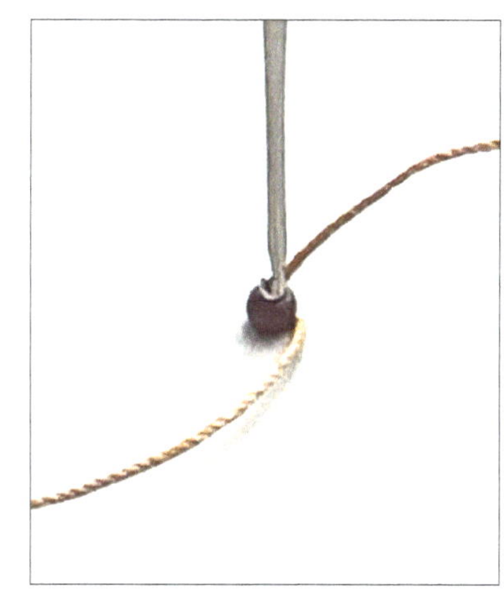

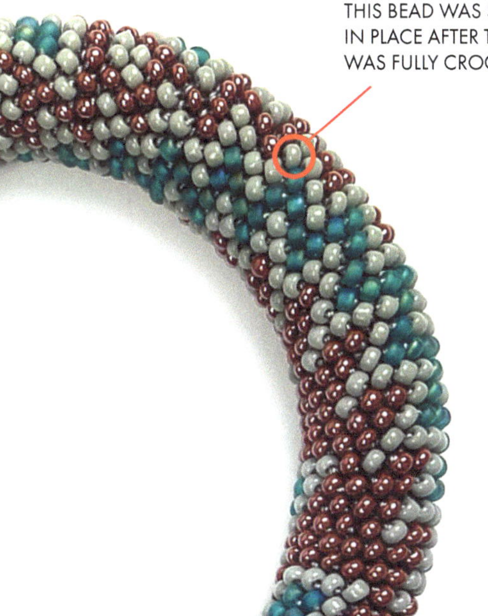

You didn't place a bead in a stitch OR you placed two beads instead of one.

It's time to *rip and redo.* Insert your hook into the stitch PRIOR to the errant stitch. Gently pull back the stitches until that point and **ascertain that the hook is in the correct** working loop by pulling GENTLY on the bead of the previous stitch. If the stitch holds, you're good to go.

If you don't test the loop and proceed with the incorrect loop, everything you've crocheted before that stitch will ravel out with the slightest pull. After crocheting a round or so, check that your pattern is lining up correctly and that all stitches are secure.

If you've crocheted many rounds beyond a stitch without a bead, you can opt to SEW it in place with beading nylon or sewing thread, paying attention to its angle.

eurobeadcrochet.annbenson

Euro crochet patterns

Designs are organized by their circumference (the number of beaded stitches in each round) from **twelve around to twenty around**, though you can go as small as ten around and as large as forty or fifty depending on your end use AND your level of patience.

Each circumference chapter has design blanks so you can bring your own ideas to life, following the guidelines below. The blanks are positioned to show how the pattern repeats. In the **simpler patterns, one repeat** of the threading pattern is shown without bead counts or color numbers. More **complex patterns will give detailed information** on bead colors and quantity requirements.

Now go have fun!

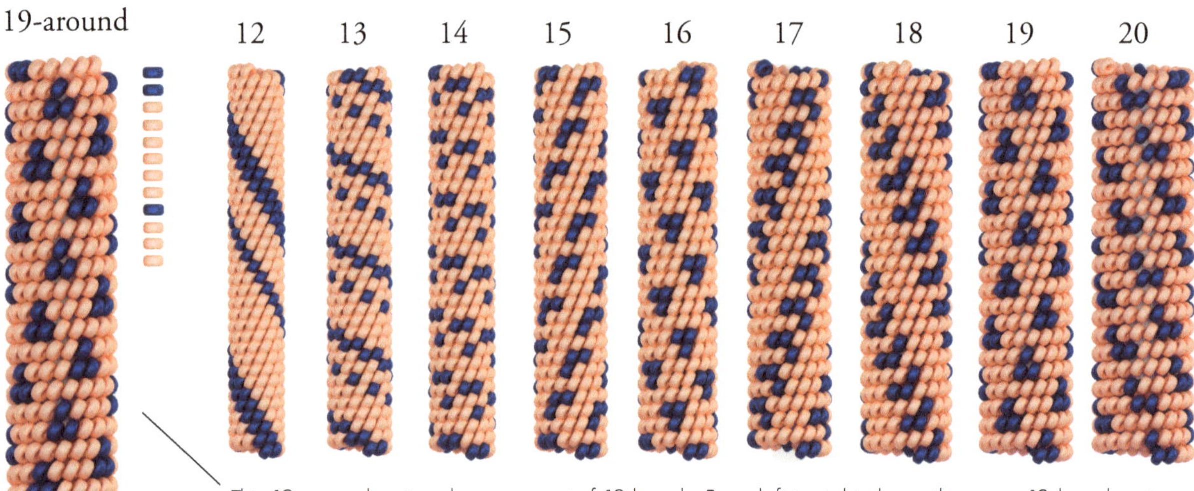

This 19-around pattern has a repeat of 12 beads. From left to right above the same 12-bead pattern is shown from 12-around to 20-around. The threading is identical, but the resulting crocheted tube has a very different appearance, both in pattern and diameter.

The graphic at right shows two full repeats of a 12-around pattern, one with beads outlined in black and one with beads outlined in red. **The red graphic is raised up by one row** so the edges of the two graphs fit together.

In this configuration, the top row of the black-lined chart flows seamlessly into the second row of the red-lined chart for a continuous design.

The pattern when threaded in full repeats will have right and left edges smoothly joined with the pattern intact. The design blanks in each section show both a single repeat and a joined repeat of the design area, by the size of the circumference.

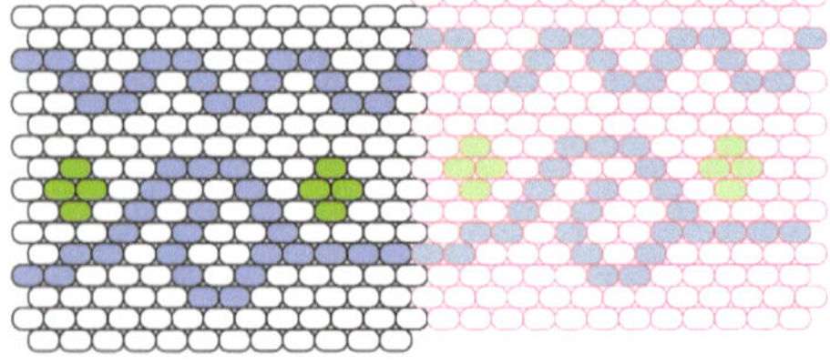

This is the first bead loaded on the thread. Threading continues left to right, top to bottom.

This narrower row (shown colored in light pink) shows the number of beads in the circumference. A design using this chart should be stitched ten-around.

This is the first bead crocheted. Your design when crocheted will be in mirror image to the chart.

16

Design blank 12-around

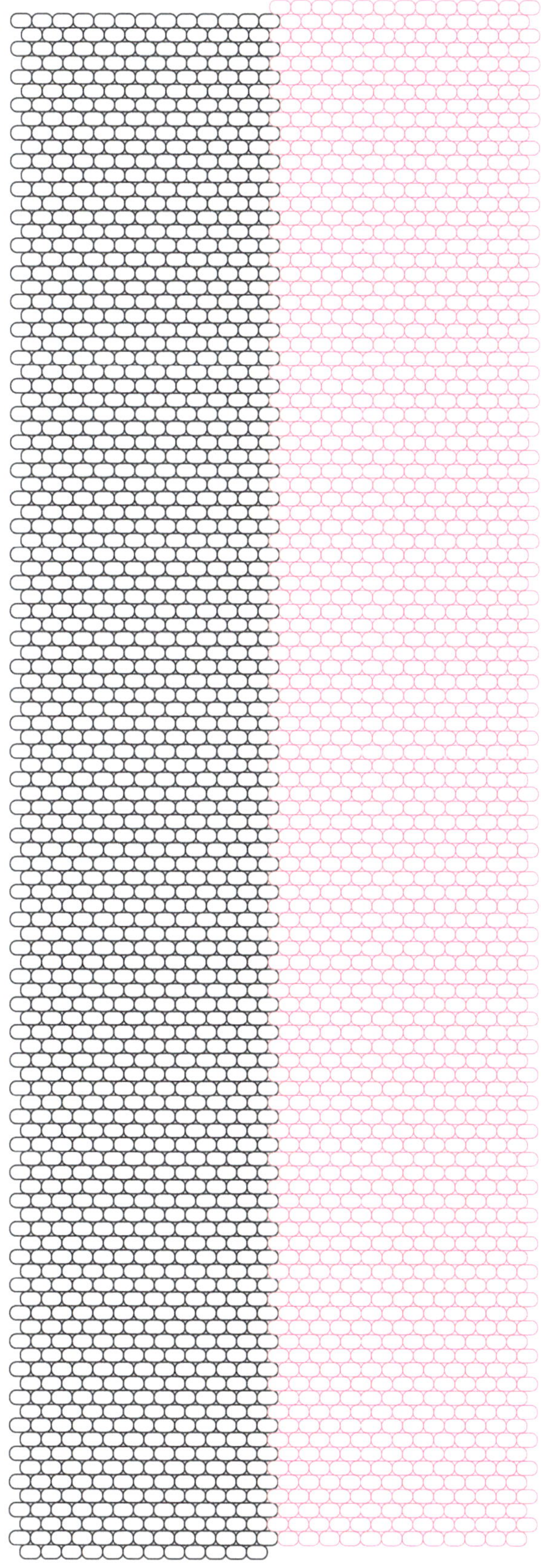

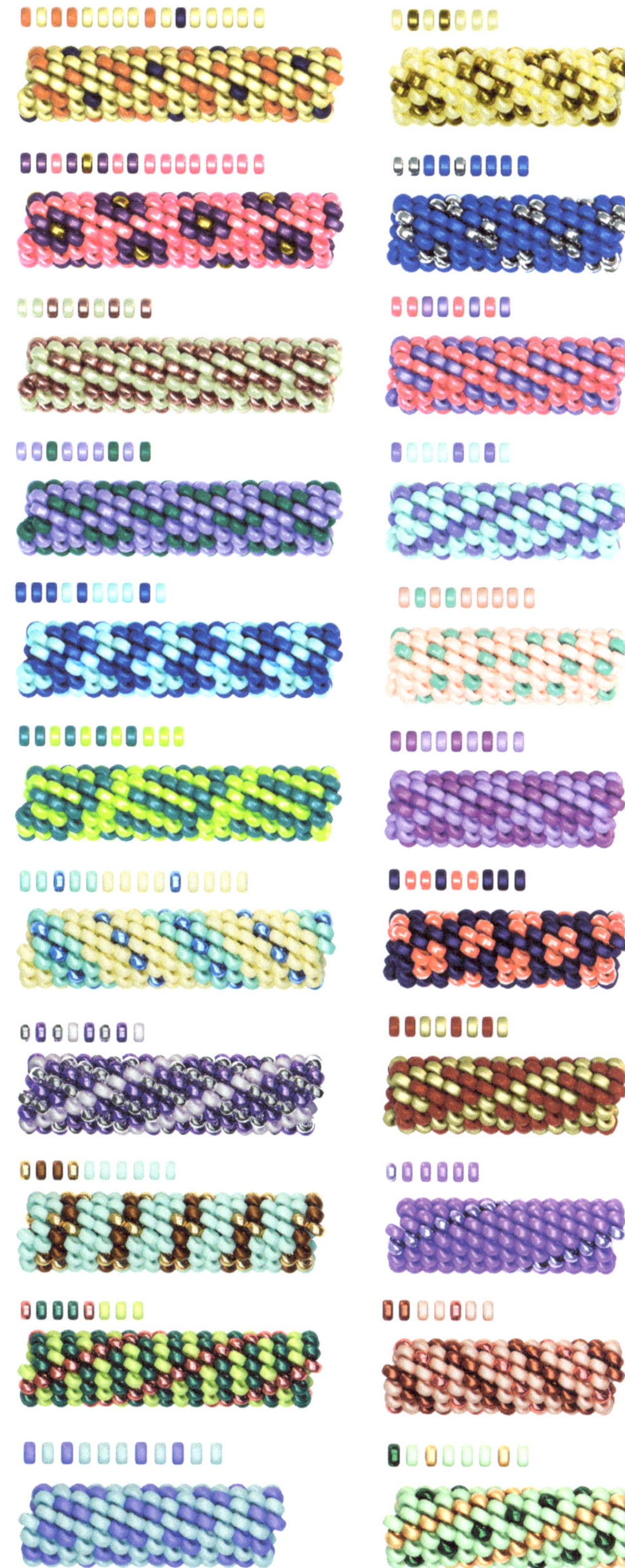

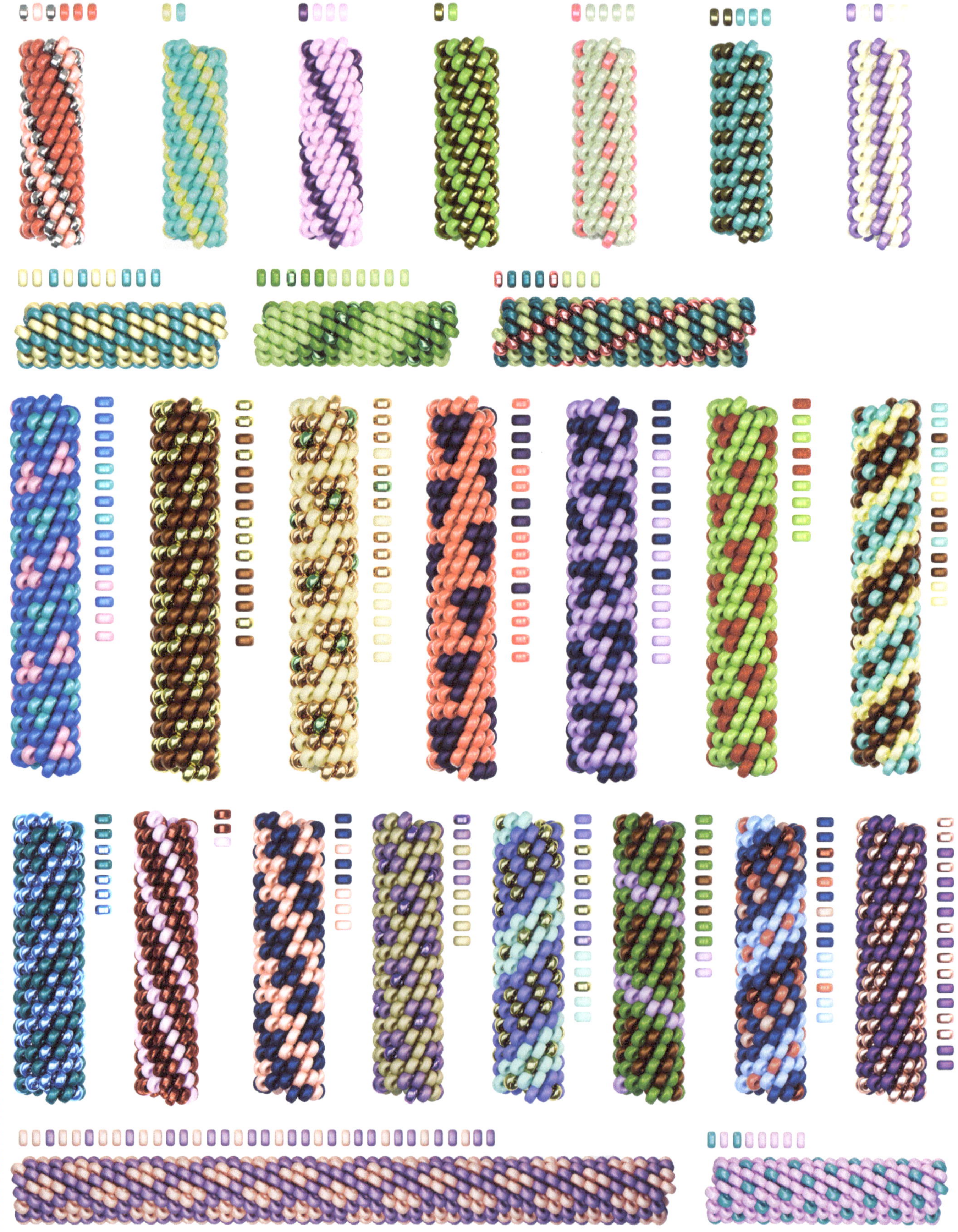

color play!

All of the **12-around designs** on this page feature the same repeating diamond pattern with the **foundational 72-bead repeat**. Small differences in how the colors are arranged (dark vs. light diamonds) and how the interiors of the diamonds are filled (solid, multicolor) can yield wonderful variation.

Each colorway includes a graphic of its own threading pattern, threaded as shown at right.

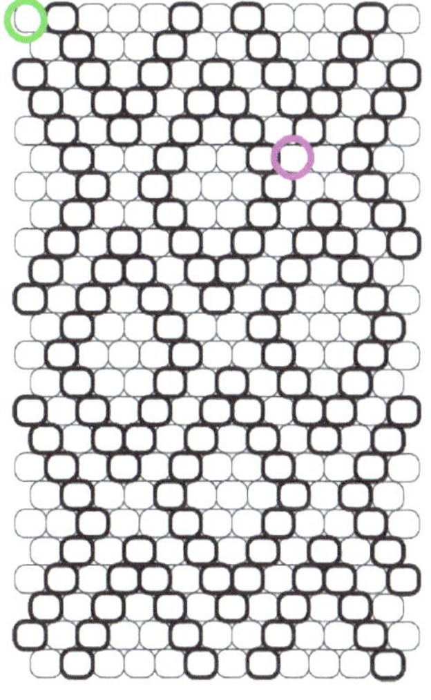

Use this design blank to create your own 12-around diamond pattern.

○ First bead of full repeat

○ Last bead of full repeat

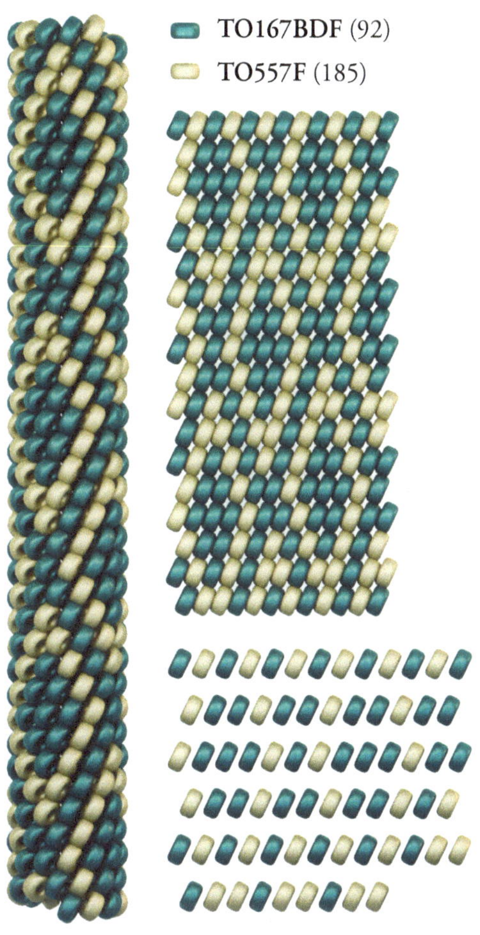

- TO167BDF (92)
- TO557F (185)

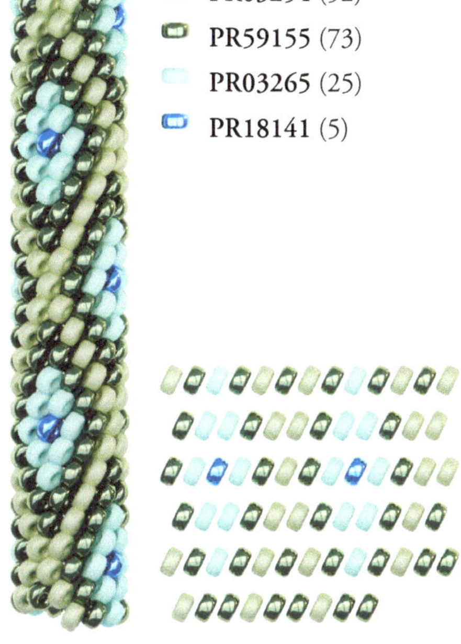

- PR03254 (52)
- PR59155 (73)
- PR03265 (25)
- PR18141 (5)

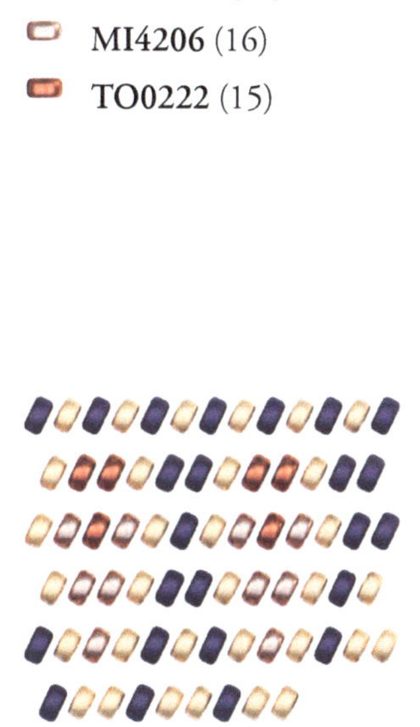

- MI0401 (56)
- PR46387 (75)
- MI4206 (16)
- TO0222 (15)

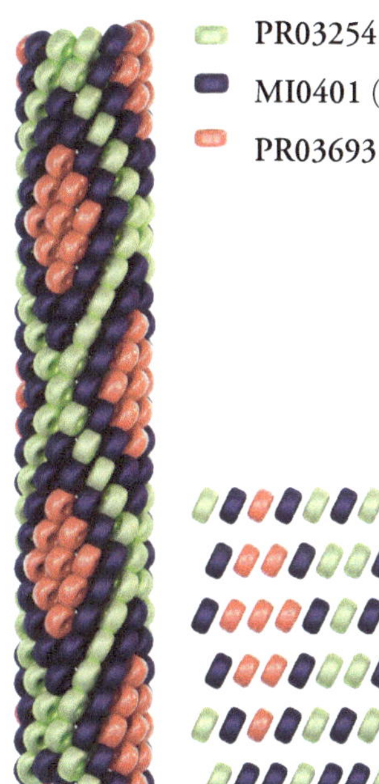

- PR03254 (54)
- MI0401 (75)
- PR03693 (39)

Design blank 13-around

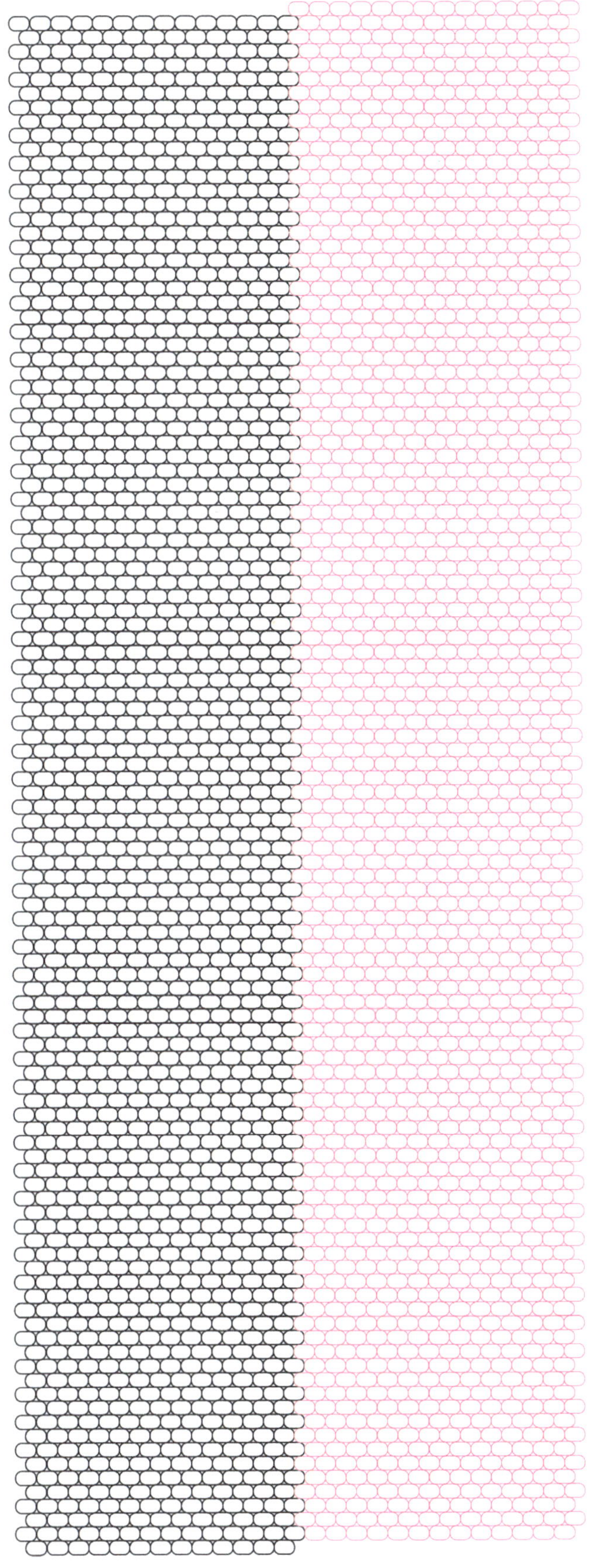

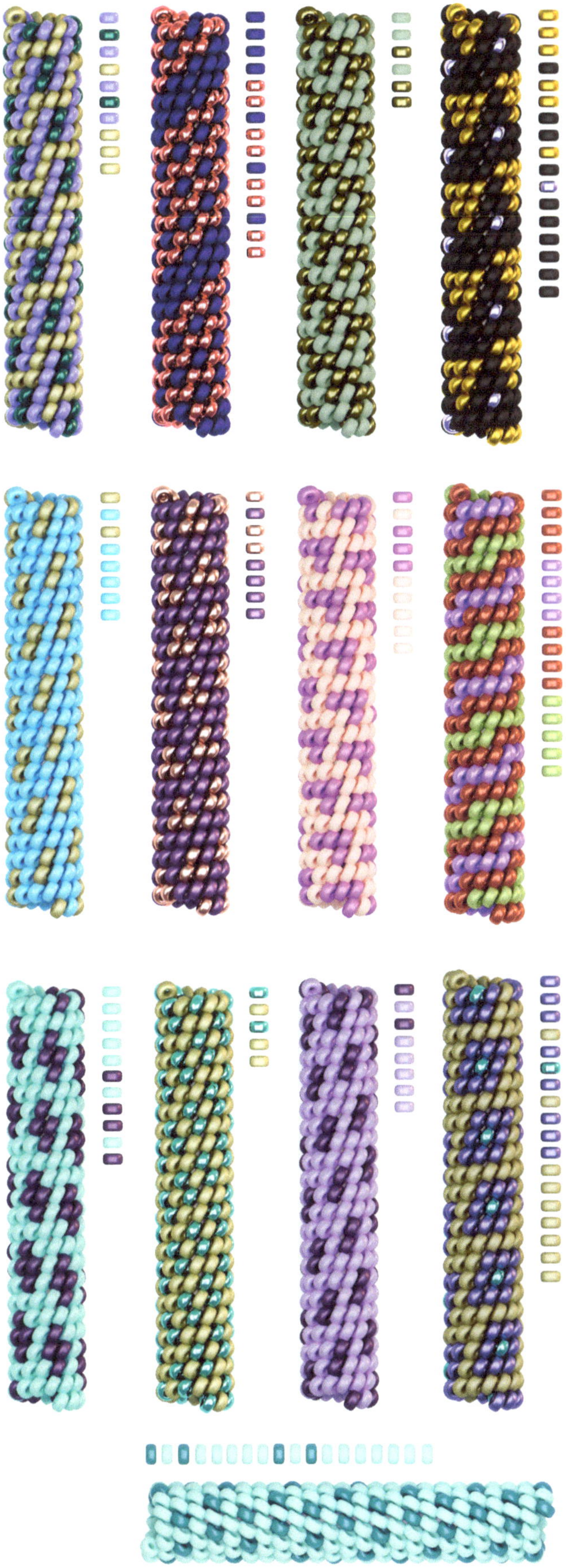

21

14-around patterns

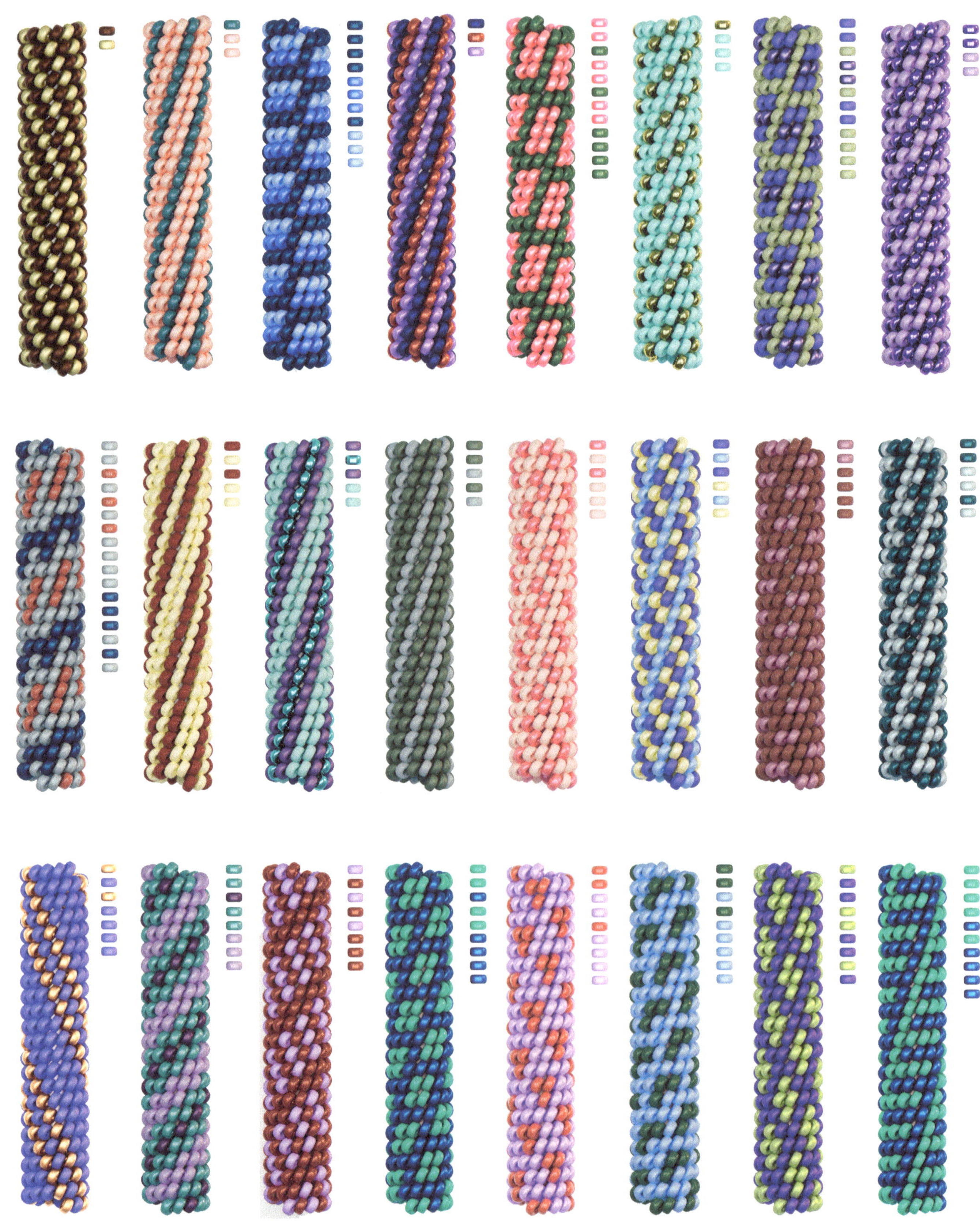

- **MI2028** matte light aqua (79)
- **MI147FR** matte aqua AB (86)
- **MI2066** dark matte aqua iris (33)
- First bead of full repeat
- Last bead of full repeat

One pattern repeat = 66 beads

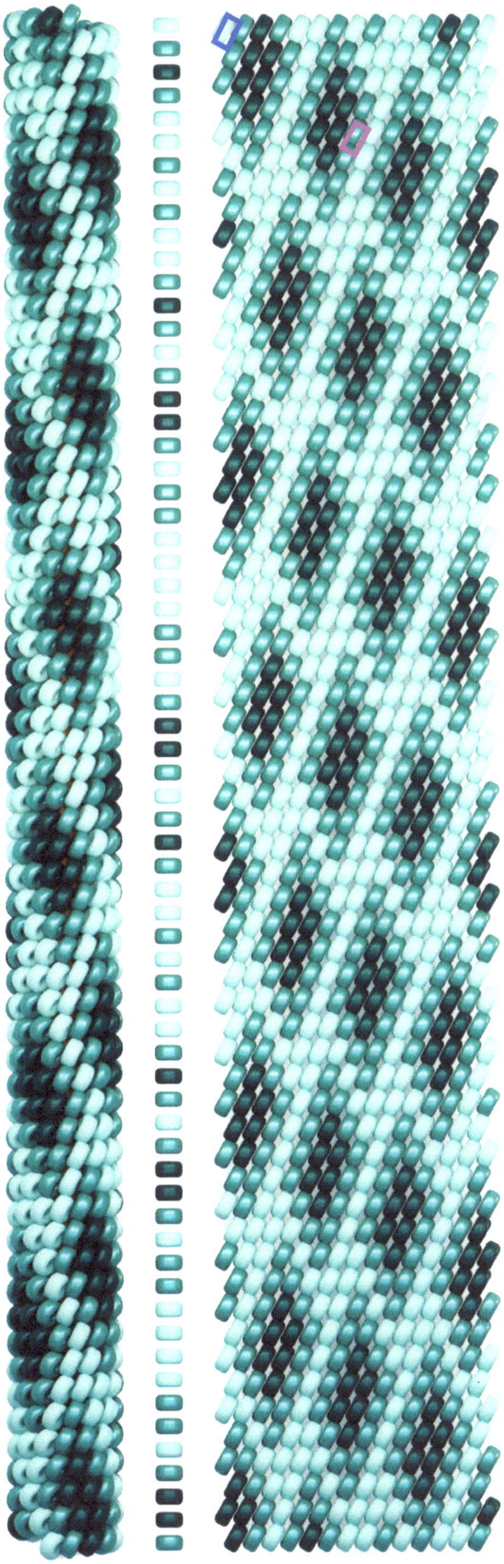

- **PR13780** opaque deep brown (90)
- **PR13600** opaque medium brown (30)
- **MI4456** opaque ochre (16)
- **MI2021** matte cream (85)
- First bead of full repeat
- Last bead of full repeat

One pattern repeat = 48 beads

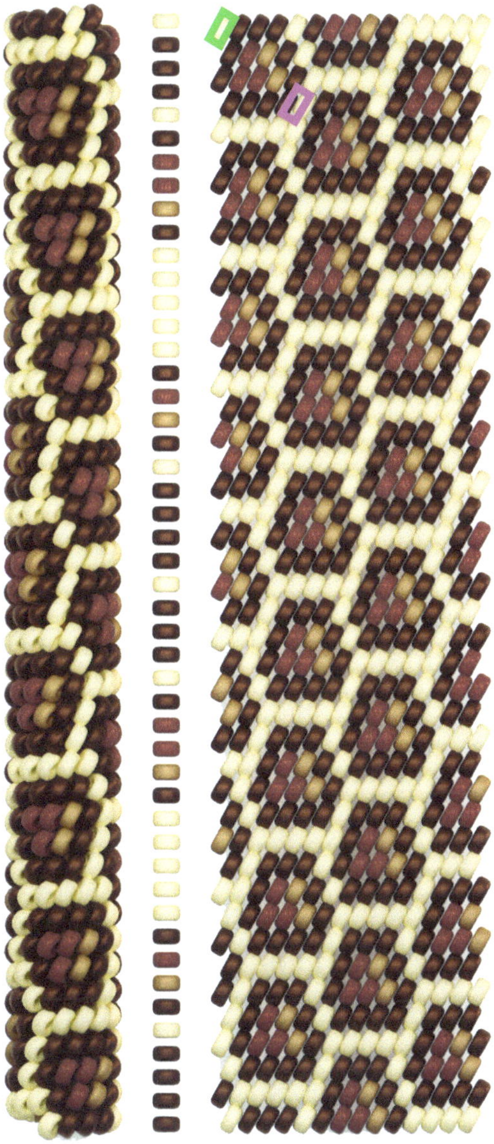

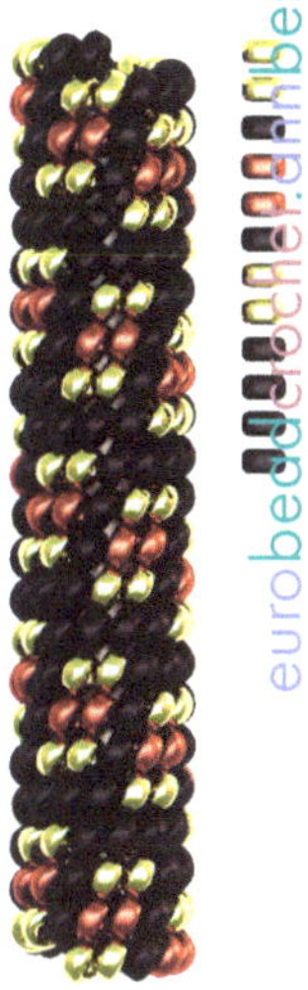

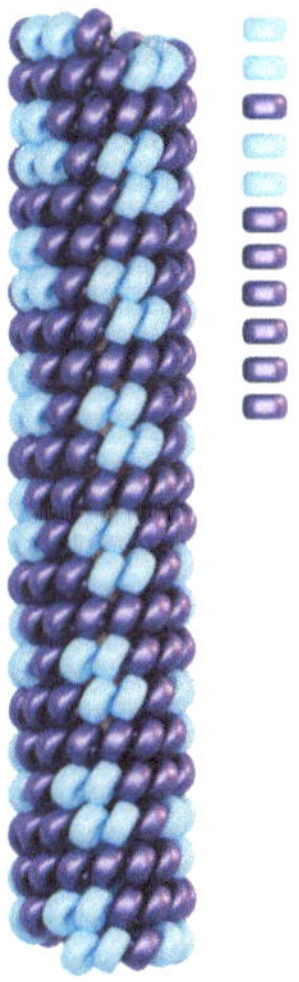

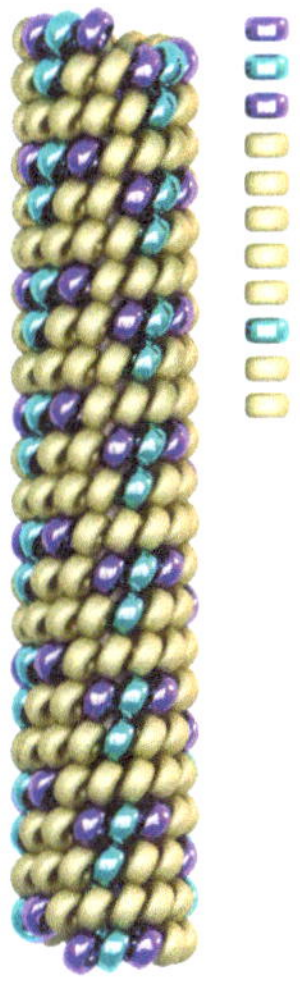

14-around patterns

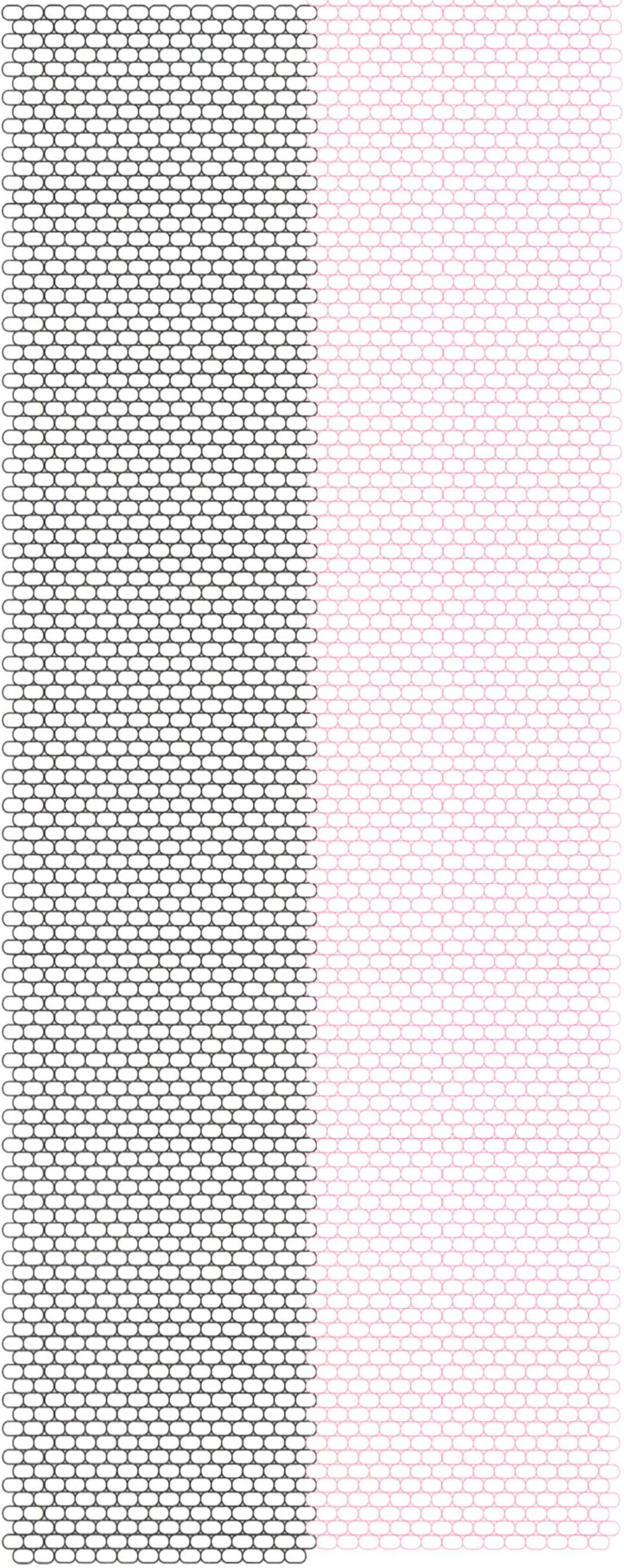

Design blank 14-around

One pattern repeat = 225 beads

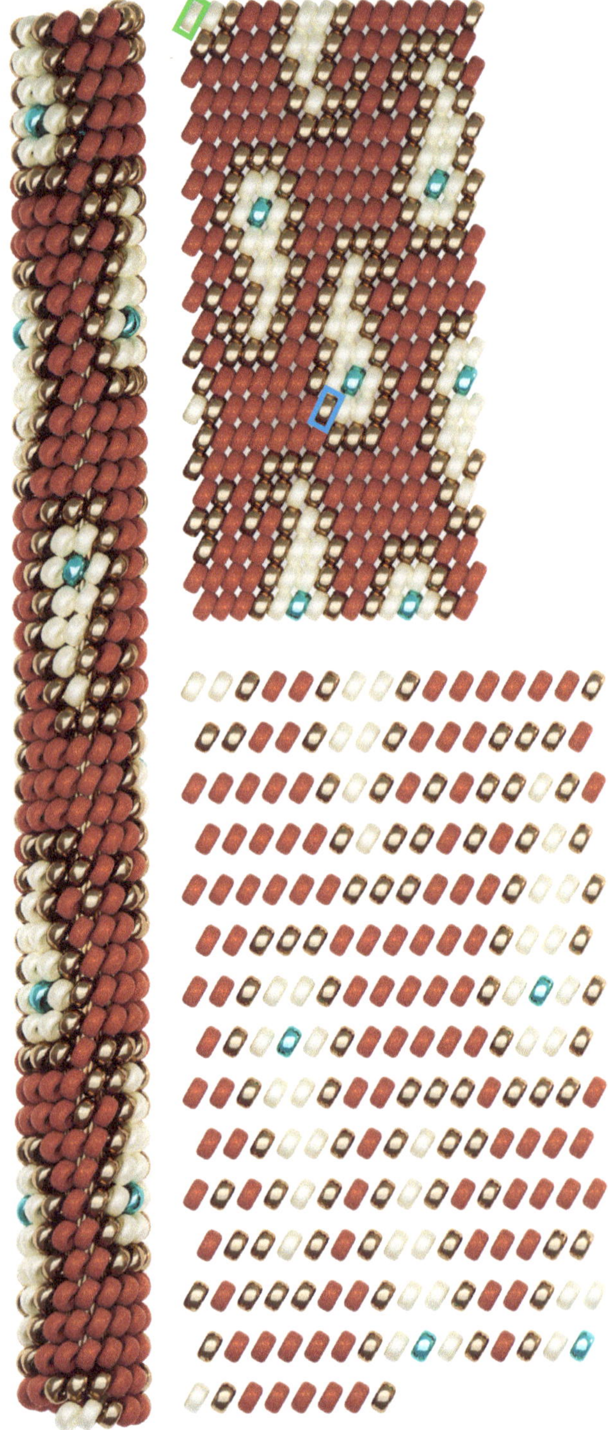

- **PR93170** opaque red (103)
- **MI4206** light copper (79)
- **PR46112** cream (39)
- **PR18586** metallic aqua (3)

One pattern repeat = 160 beads

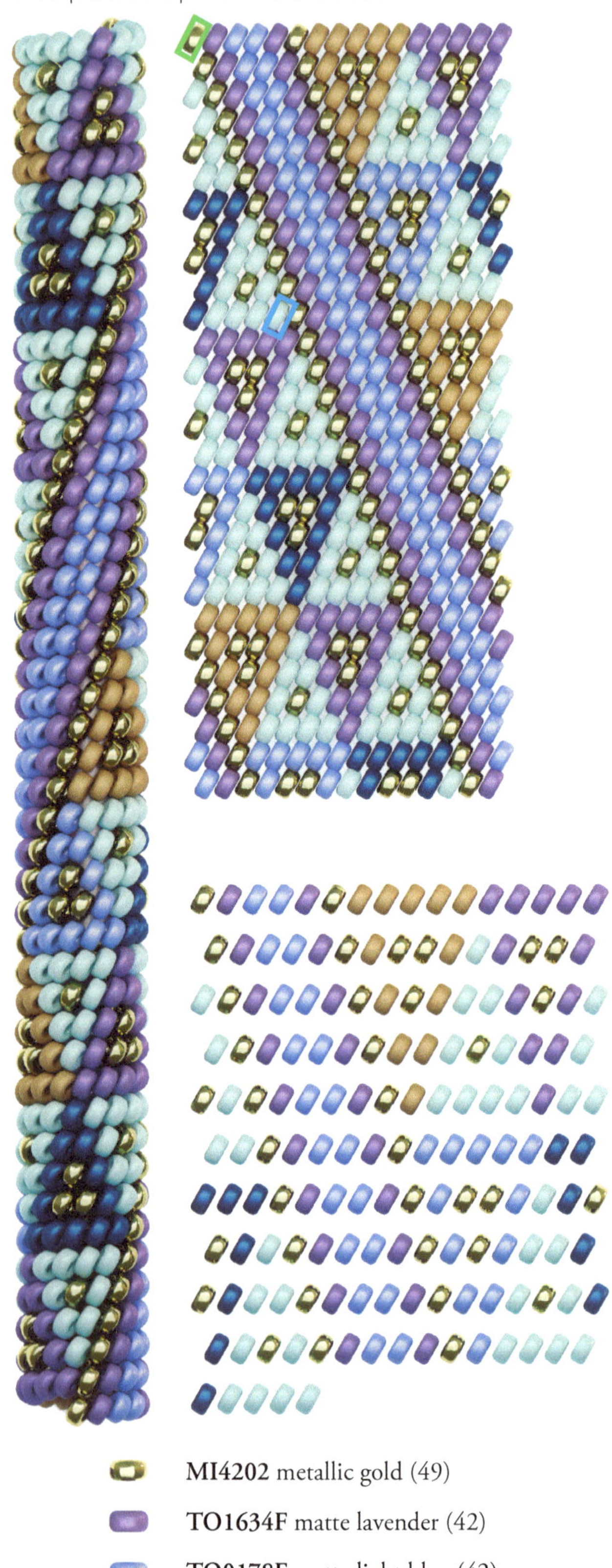

- **MI4202** metallic gold (49)
- **TO1634F** matte lavender (42)
- **TO0178F** matte light blue (42)
- **PR03652** ochre (42)
- **PR03264** light matte aqua (49)
- **MI4485** duracoat dark aqua (42)

Design blank 15-around

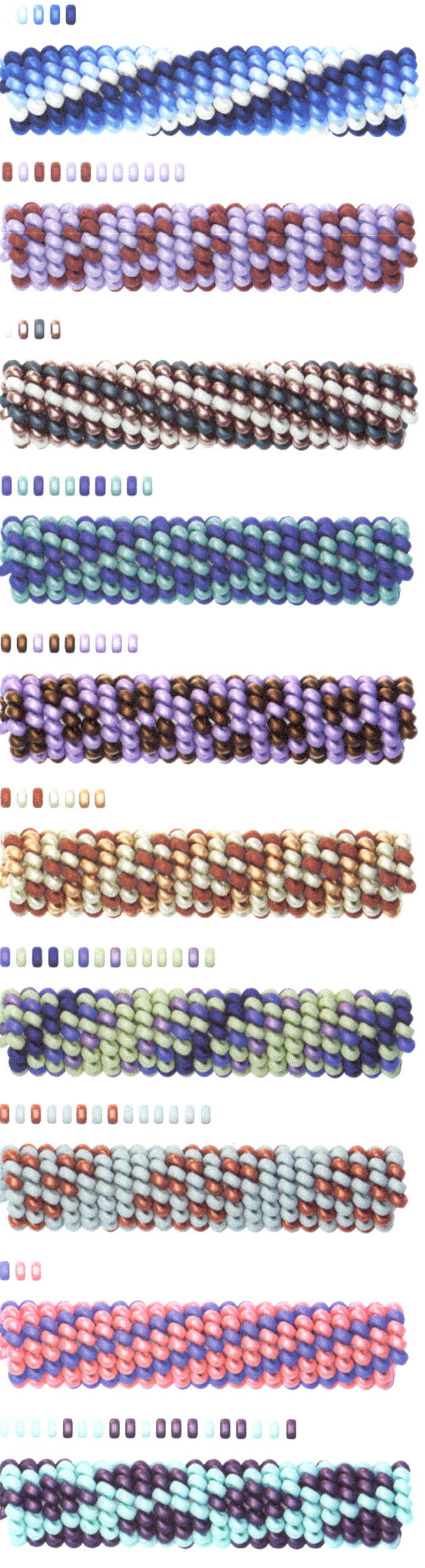

15-around patterns

All four of the 15-around patterns below have 41-bead repeats and are based on the same hexagon shape. These patterns offer many opportunities for color experimentation.

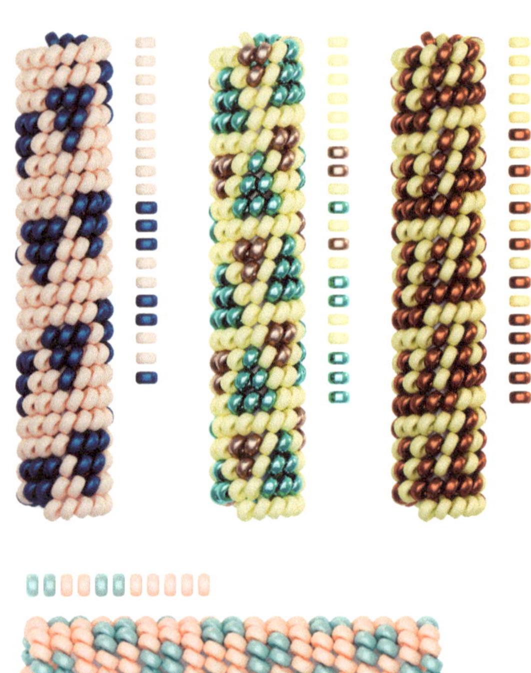

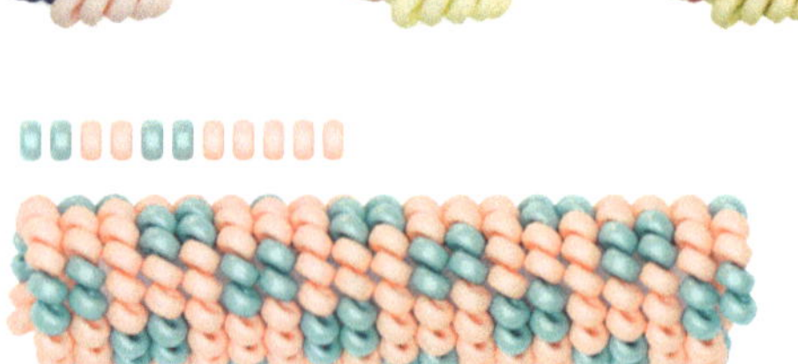

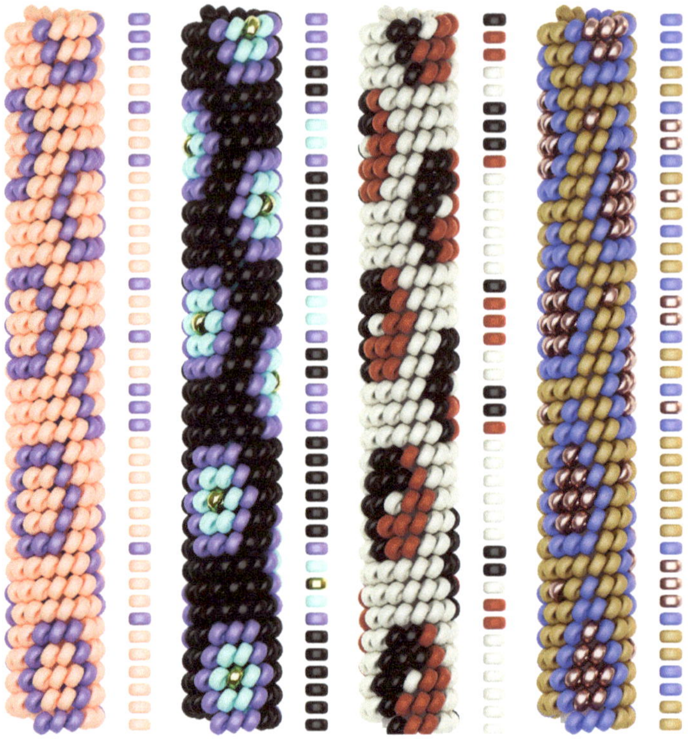

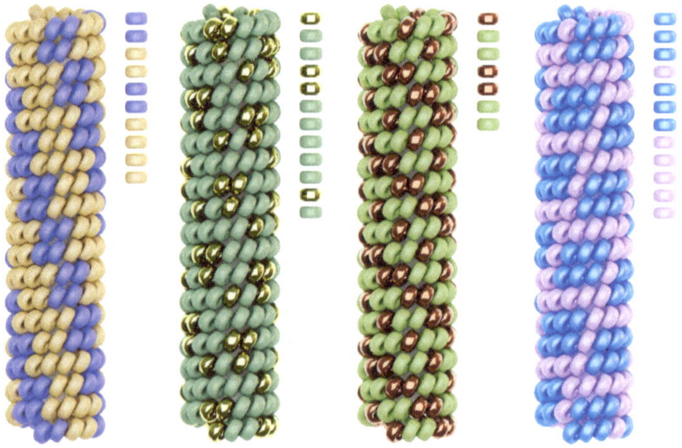

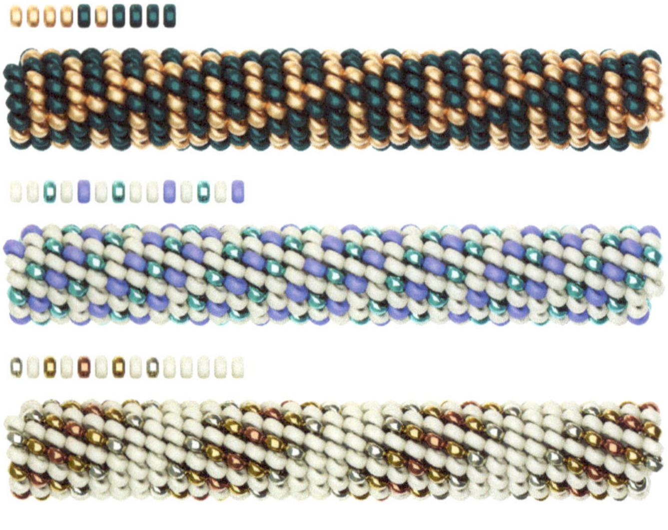

The three 15-around patterns below all have 20-bead repeats. Slight alterations in the placement of colors can make a dramatic difference in how the pattern appears when crocheted.

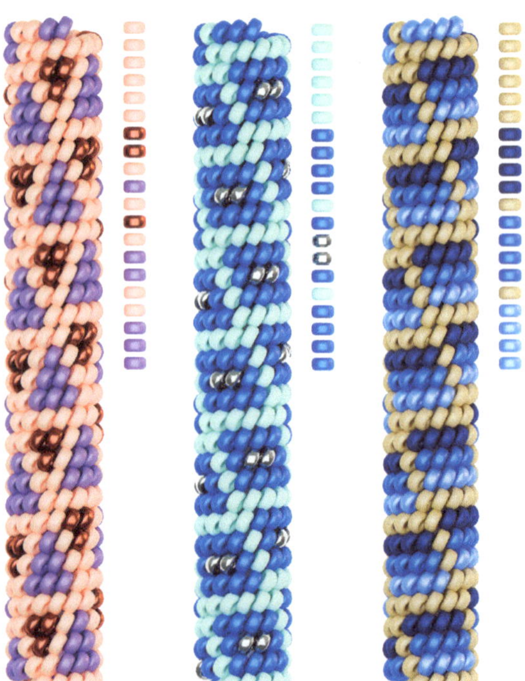

16-around patterns

One pattern repeat = 272 beads

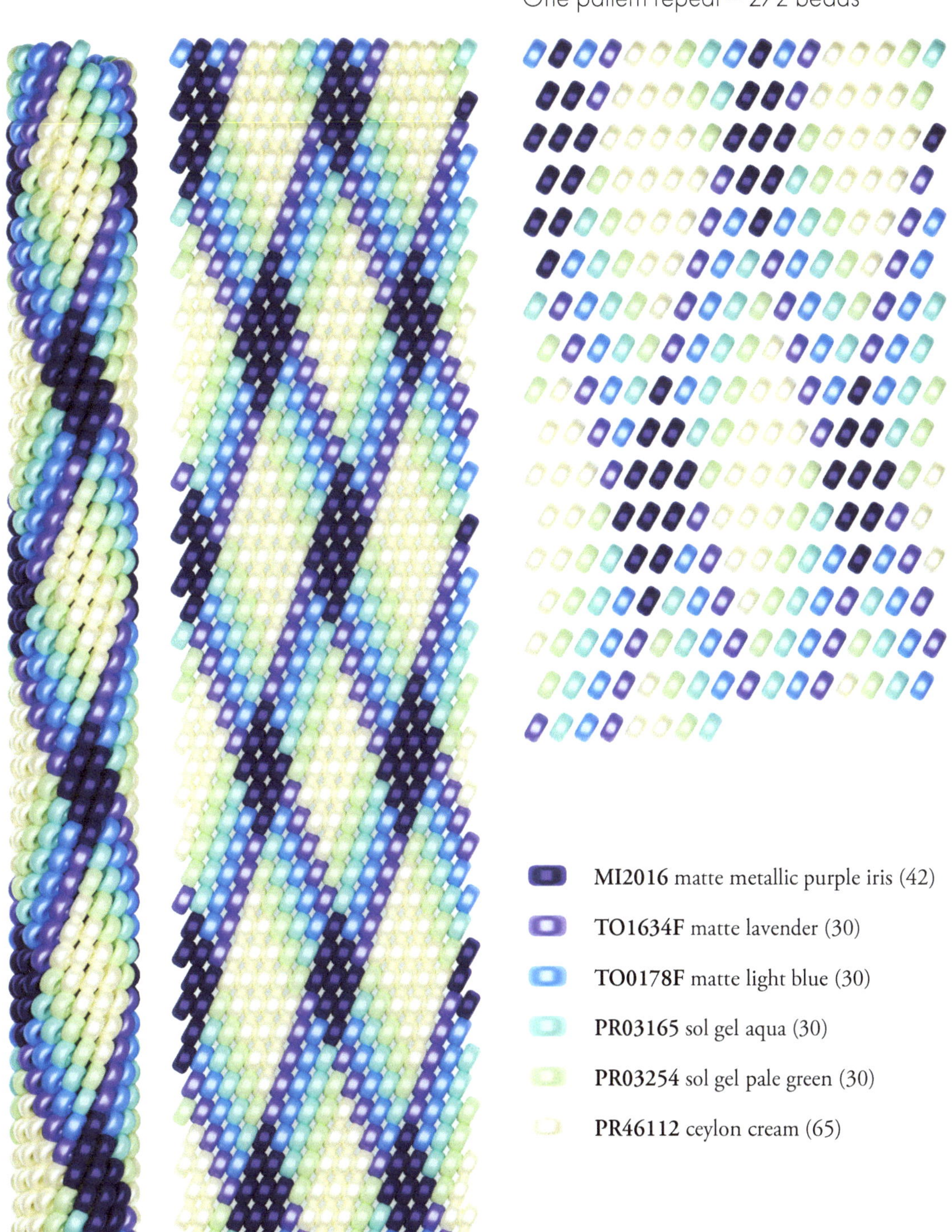

MI2016 matte metallic purple iris (42)

TO1634F matte lavender (30)

TO0178F matte light blue (30)

PR03165 sol gel aqua (30)

PR03254 sol gel pale green (30)

PR46112 ceylon cream (65)

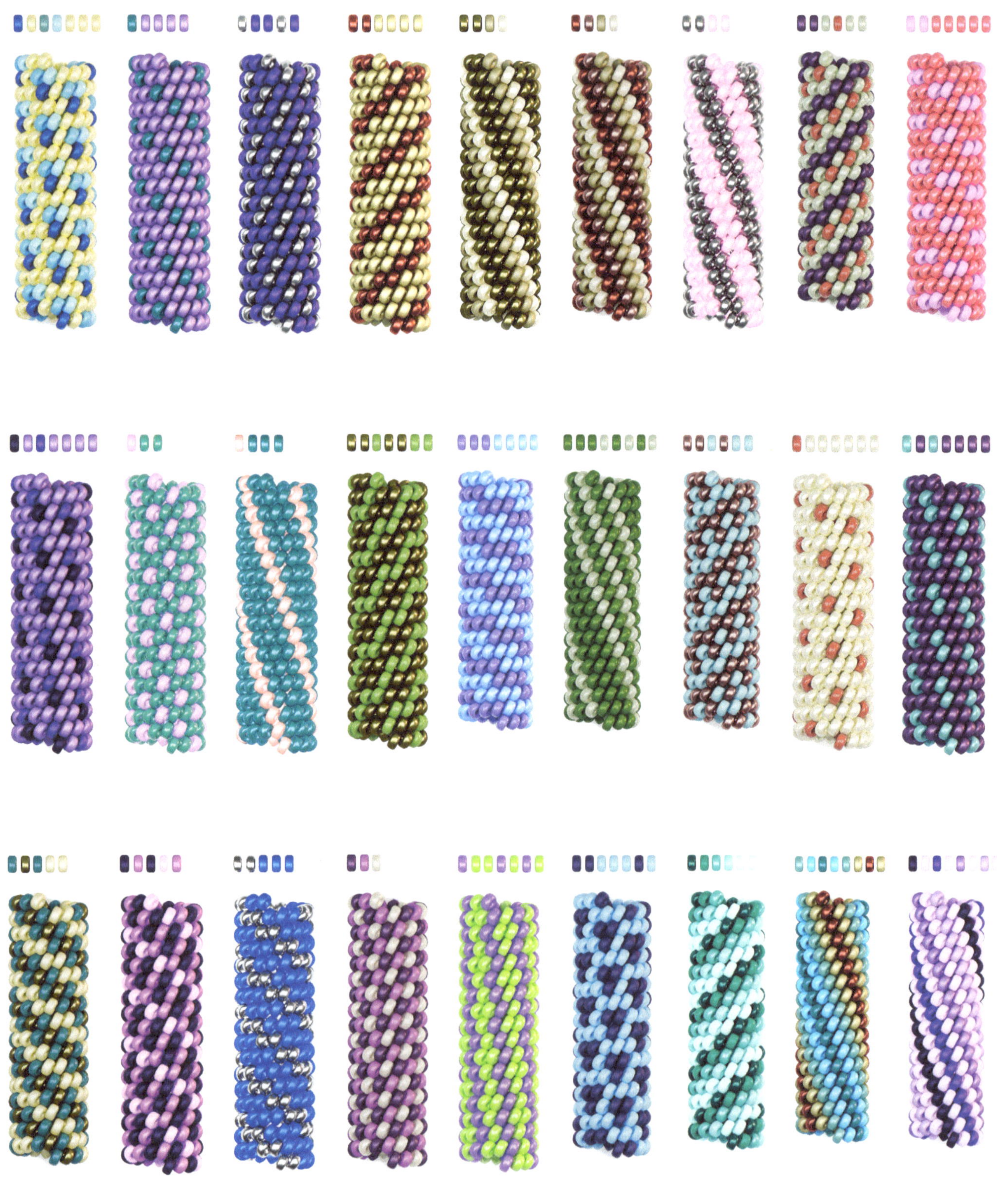

Design blank 16-around

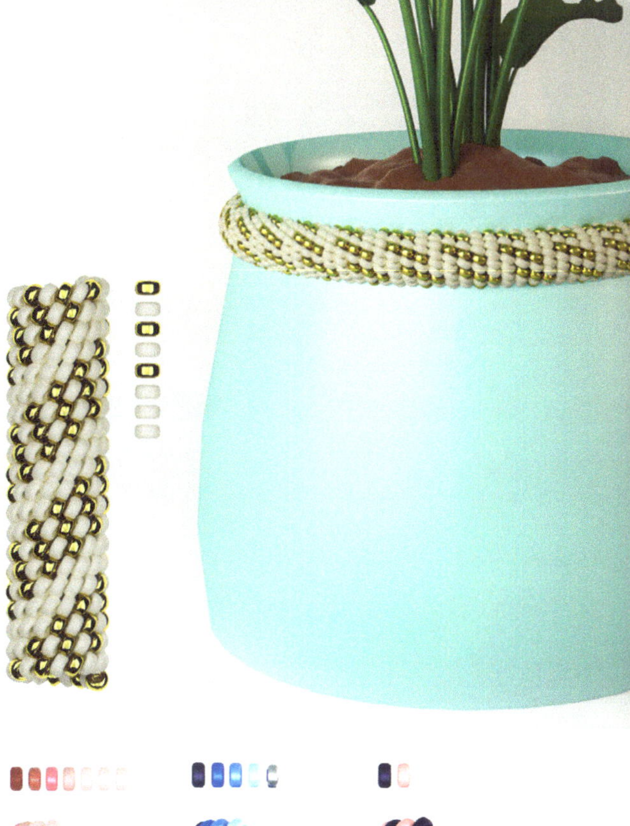

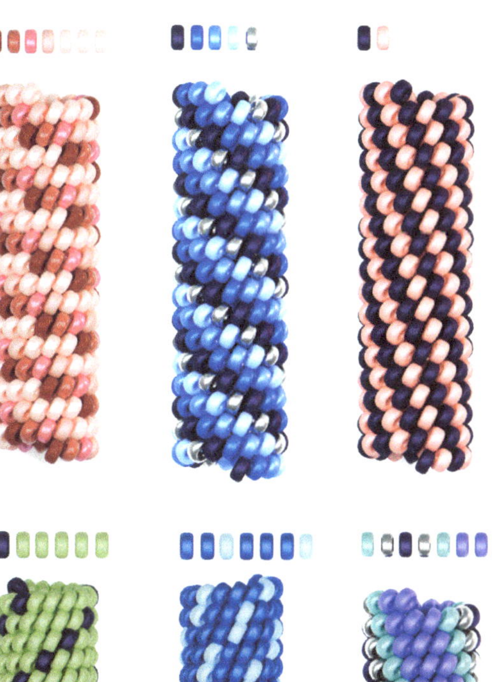

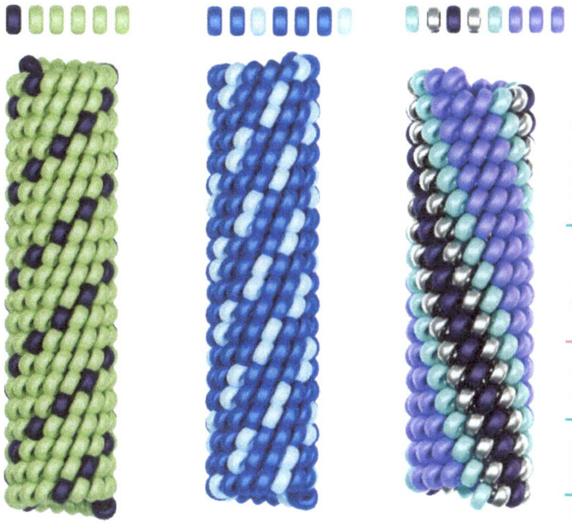

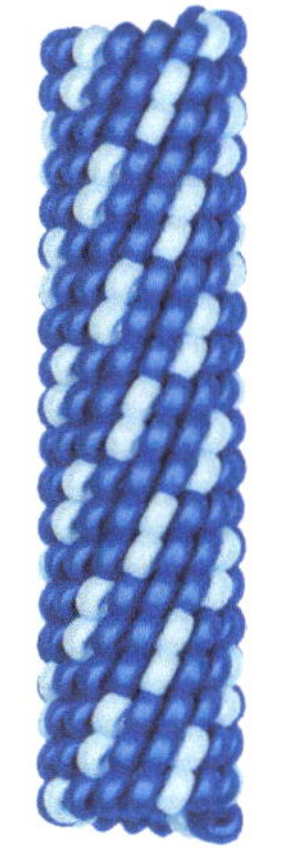

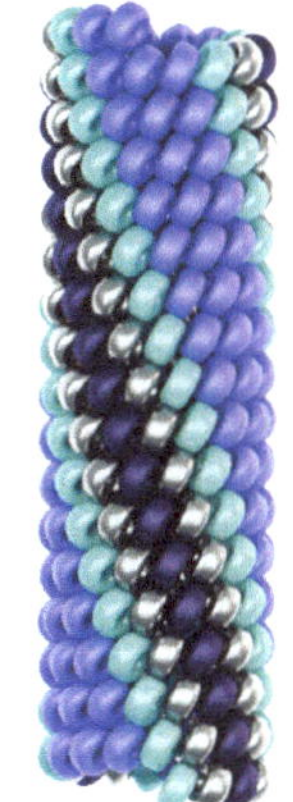

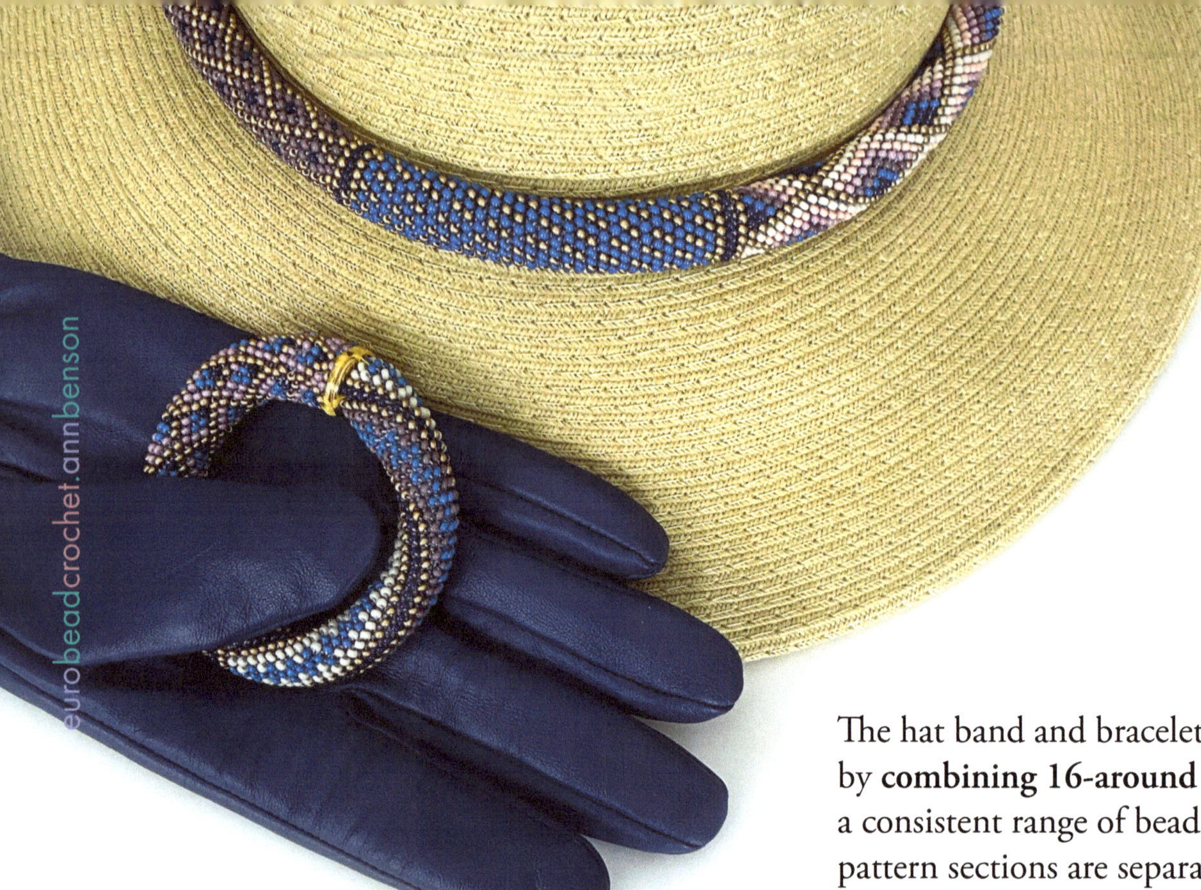

The hat band and bracelet are both created by **combining 16-around patterns** with a consistent range of bead colors. The pattern sections are separated by three-round bands with one color sandwiched between rounds of matte gold.

Both are closed with a sewn-on snap. This closure allows for the hat band to be worn as a necklace as well.

Below are the colors used consistently throughout the band and bracelet. Some of the patterns only use two colors, while one uses all seven. Specific colors used are indicated within the pattern and above or beside it.

Needed amounts should be determined according to the length of your planned piece.

- **PR01710** matte gold
- **MI0491** opaque cream
- **PR38394** lustered dusty pink
- **PR23030** opaque light amethyst
- **MI0411** opaque amethyst
- **PR33220** opaque marine blue
- **PR33070** lustered deep navy

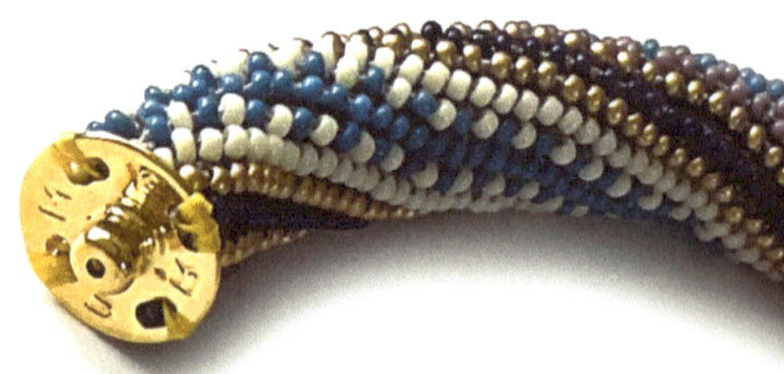

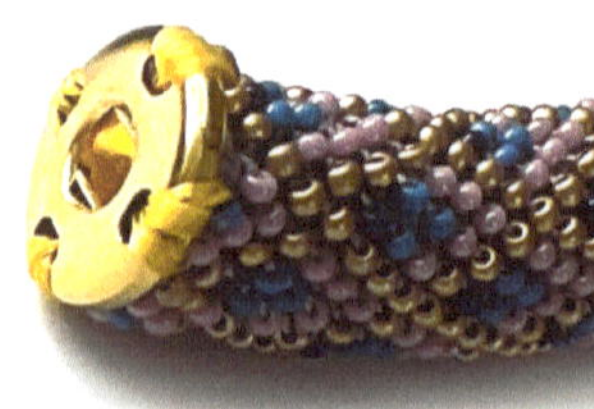

A hat trick, 16-around.

One pattern repeat = 128 beads

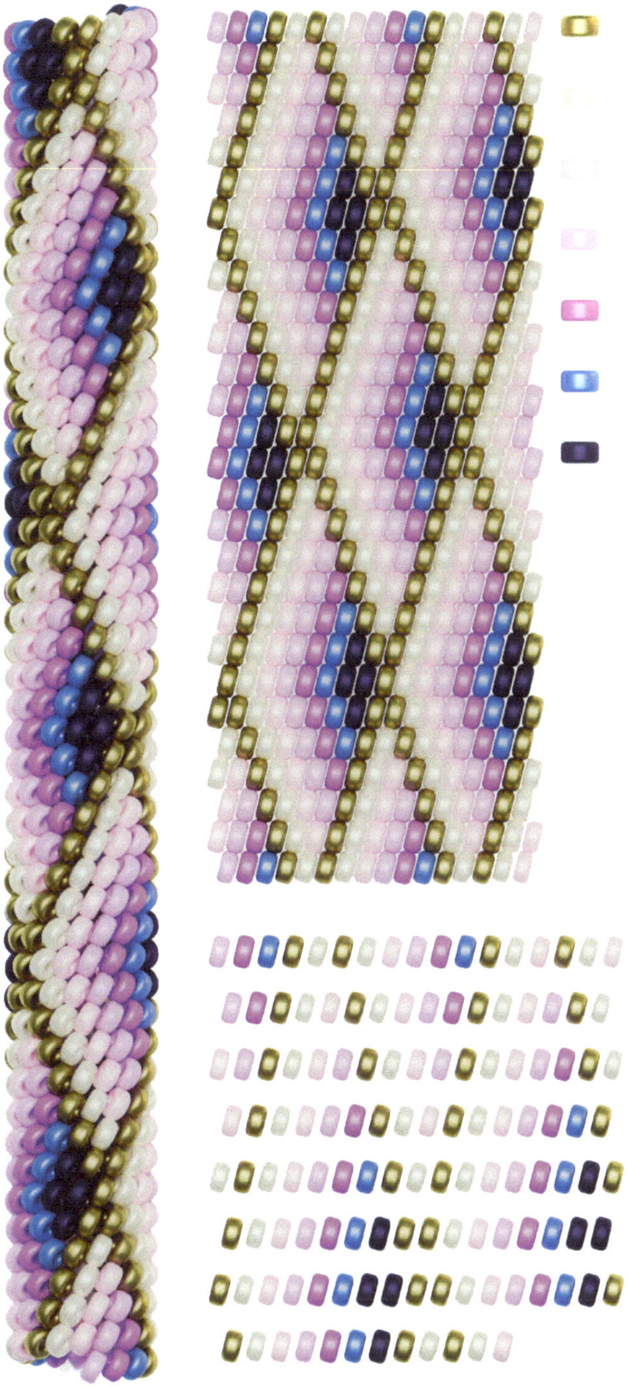

One pattern repeat = 64 beads

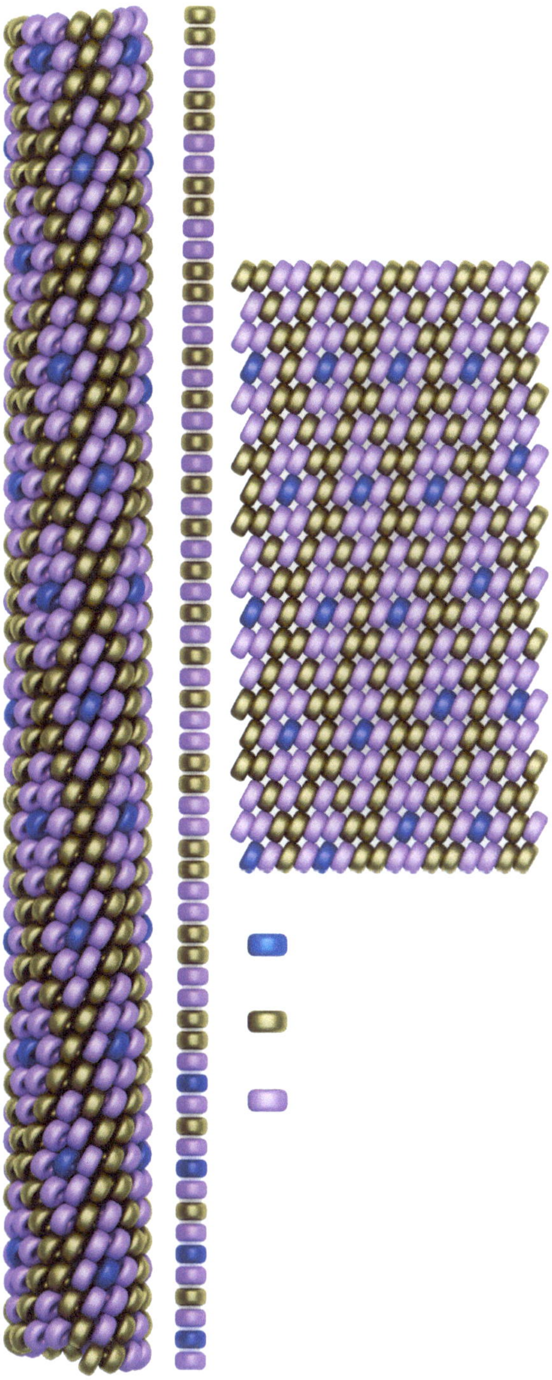

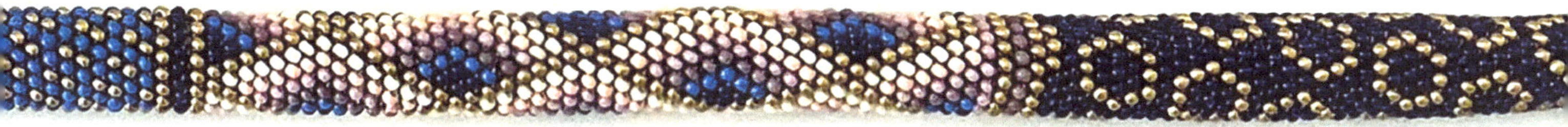

One pattern repeat = 64 beads

One pattern repeat = 32 beads

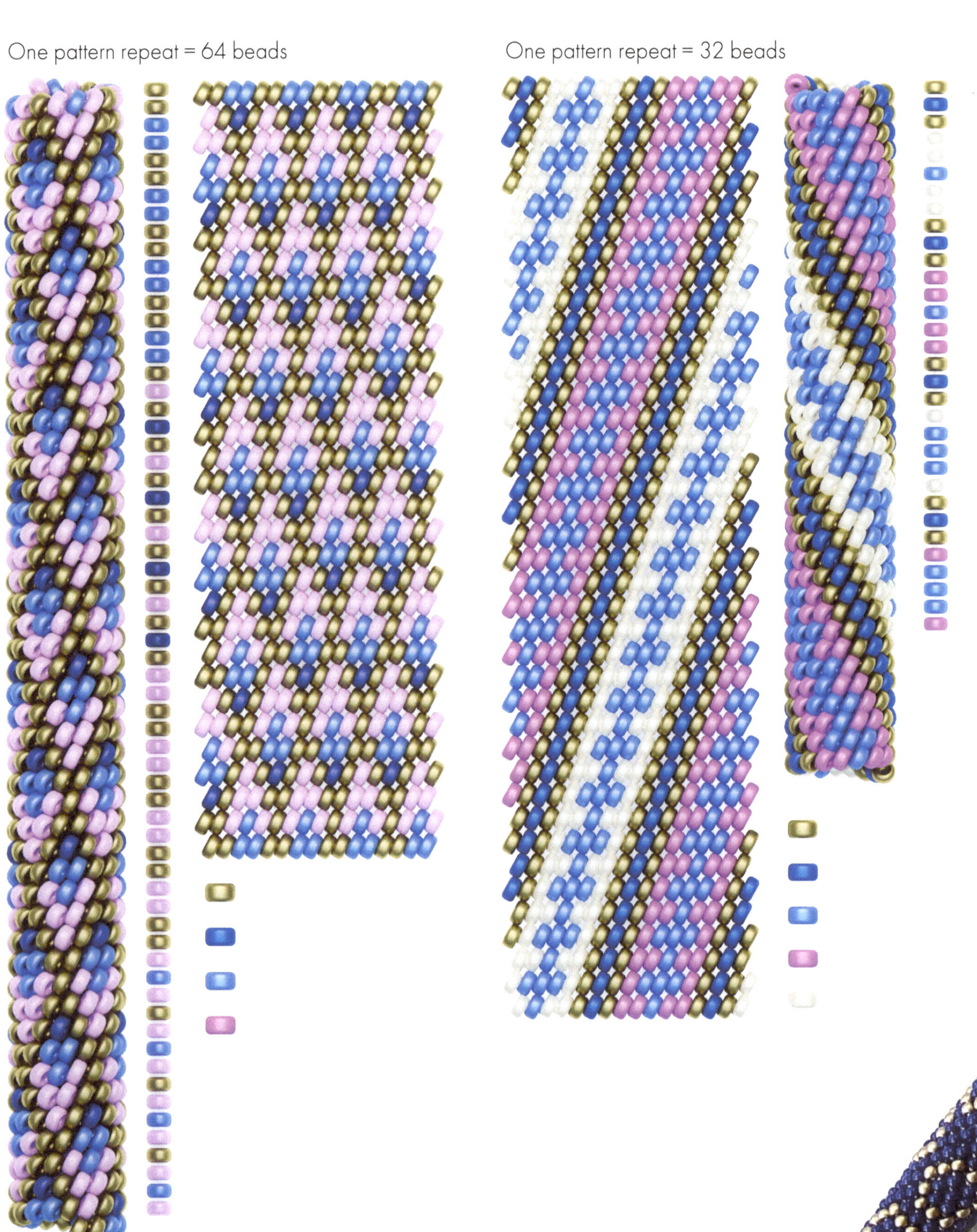

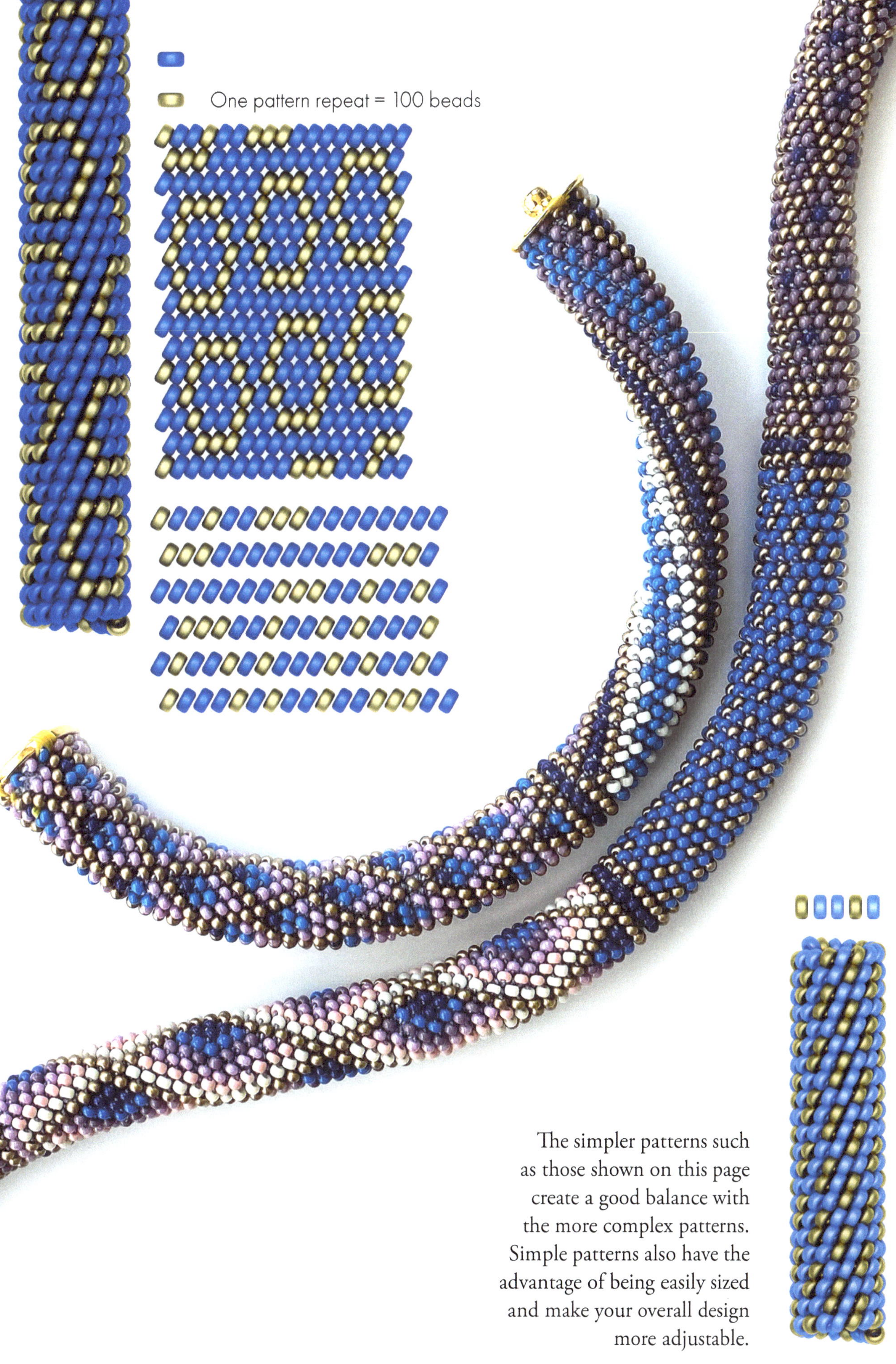

The simpler patterns such
as those shown on this page
create a good balance with
the more complex patterns.
Simple patterns also have the
advantage of being easily sized
and make your overall design
more adjustable.

35

17-around patterns

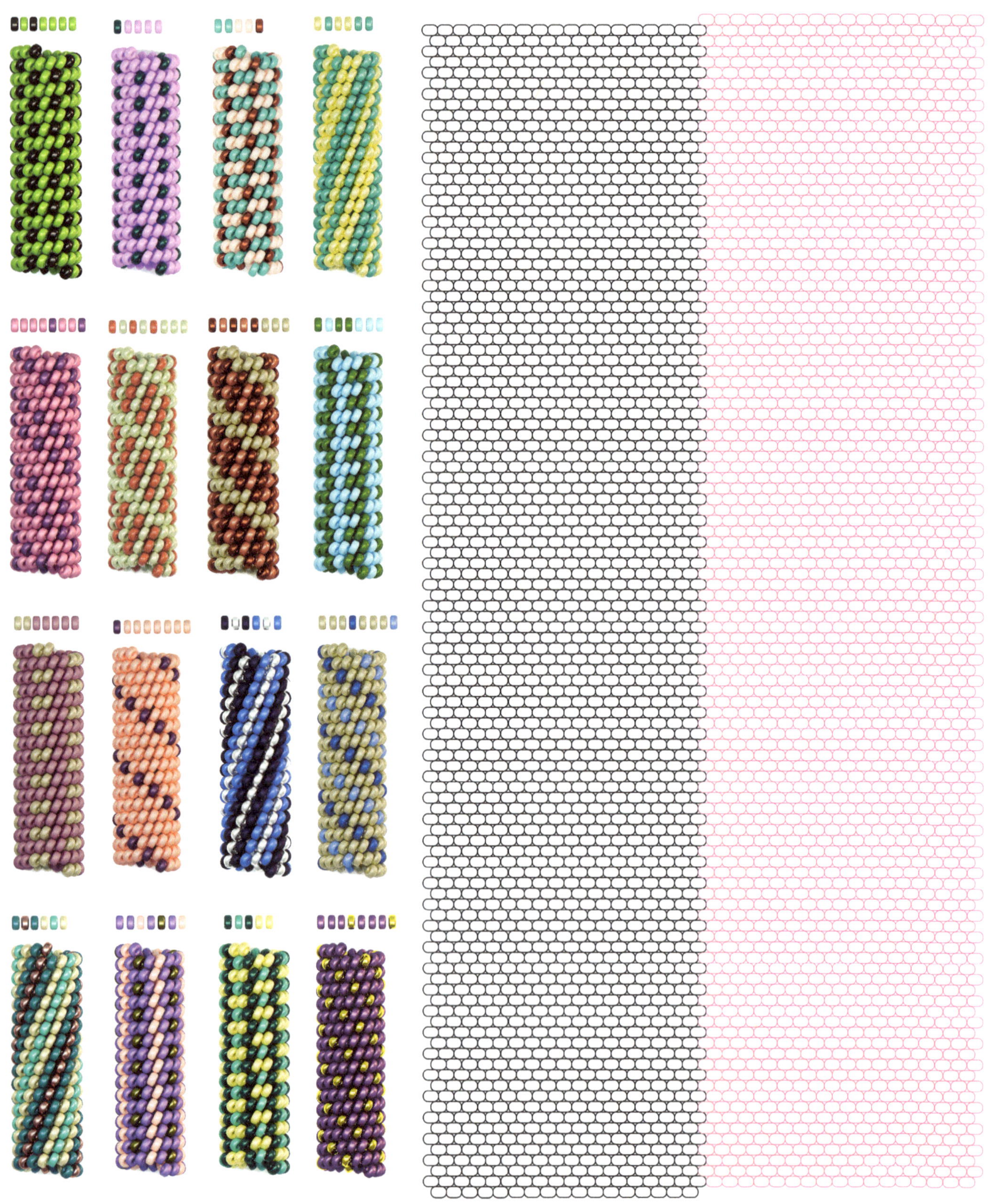

Design blank 17-around

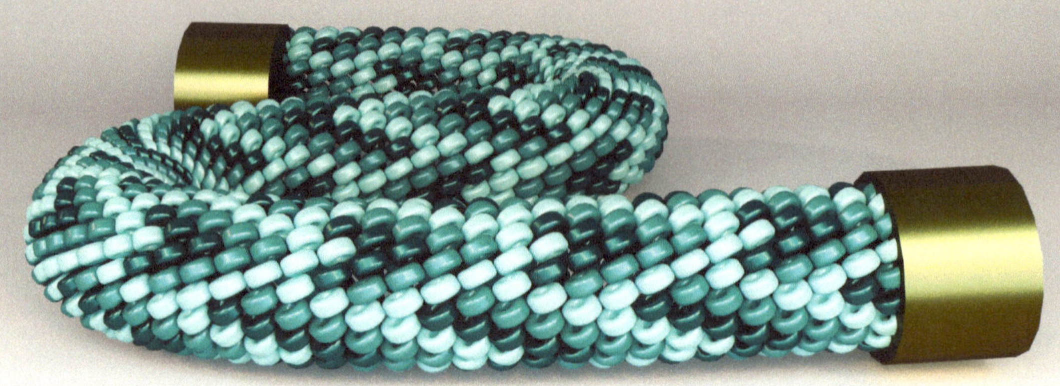

One pattern repeat = 100 beads

MI2028 matte seafoam (105)

MI2066 matte opaque dark green (66)

MI4477 opaque spruce (86)

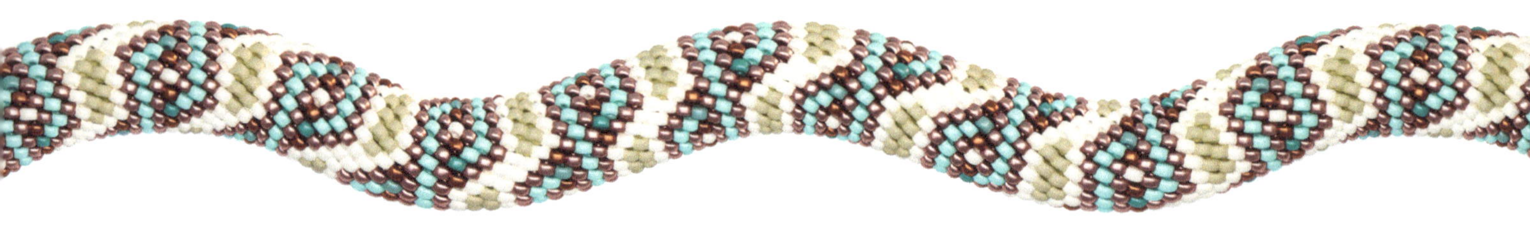

One pattern repeat = 64 beads

MI4206 duracoat copper (84)

MI0491 opaque cream (66)

MI0493 opaque pear (31)

PR46055 opaque light turquoise (43)

TO0222 dark metallic copper (15)

PR53233 opaque turquoise (7)

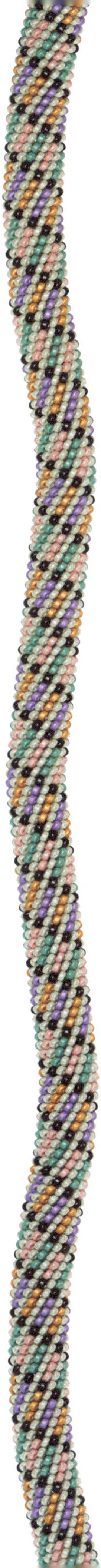

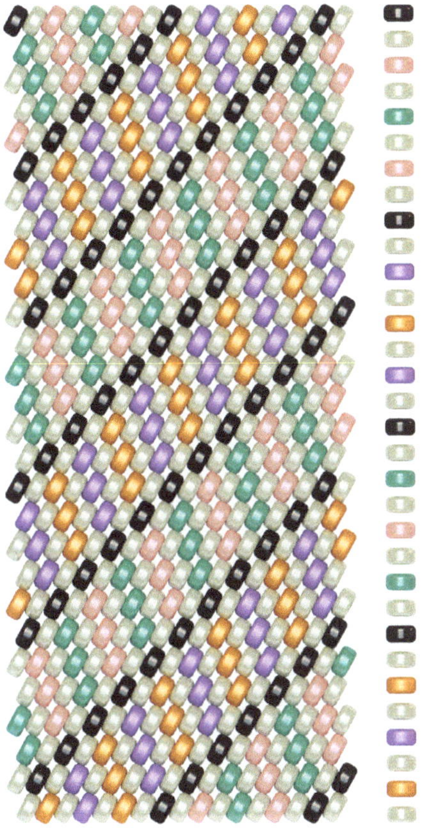

One pattern repeat = 32 beads

PR03212 terra light rose (23)

MI2028 matte opaque seafoam (23)

M0491 opaque cream (50)

MI0401F opaque matte jet (30)

PR73030M matte medium amethyst (23)

MI4454 duracoat pumpkin (23)

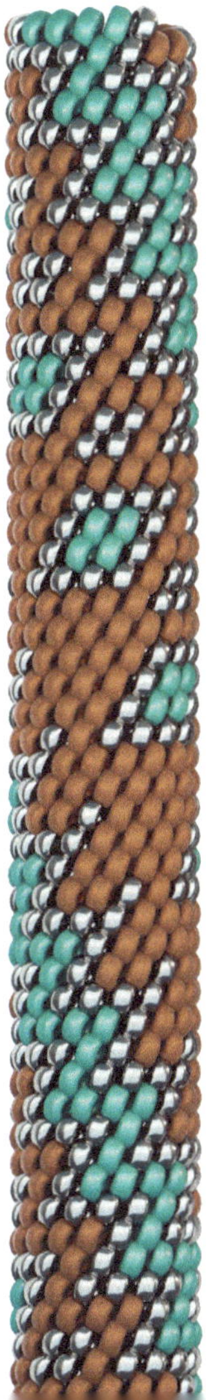

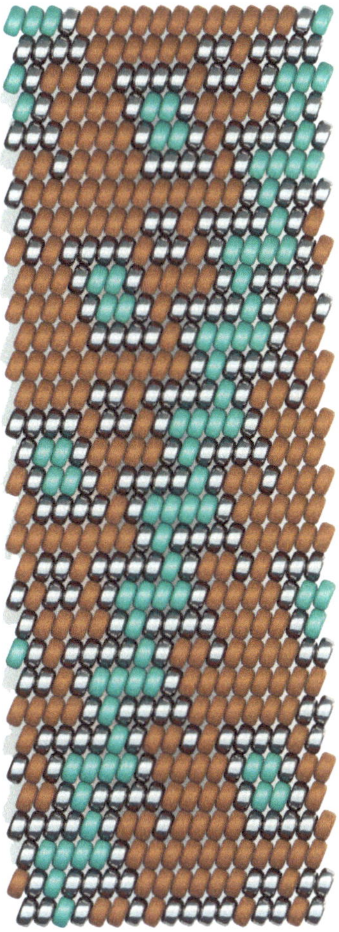

PR13600M matte brick (107)

M4201 duracoat silver (102)

MI2028 matte opaque seafoam (36)

One pattern repeat = 101 beads

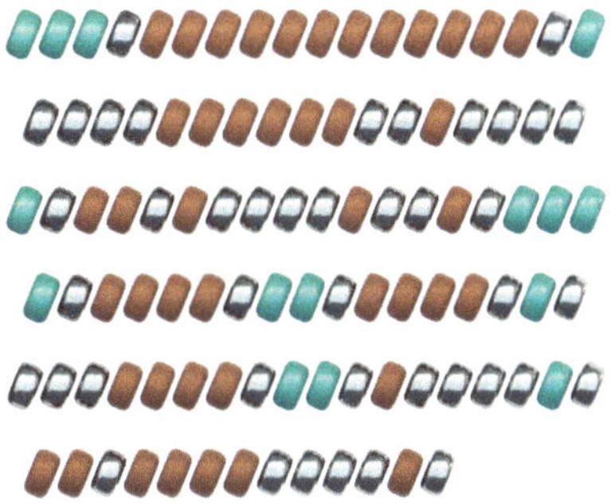

39

Fun with texture!

No matter how many beads are in your circumference, you can **add texture by varying the size** of the beads within your pattern.

This 16-around design has a 23-bead repeat with a section of three different-sized beads. With textured patterns, it's a good idea to establish your tube with the base size (in this case 11°s) for stability, and then end with a span of the same size bead.

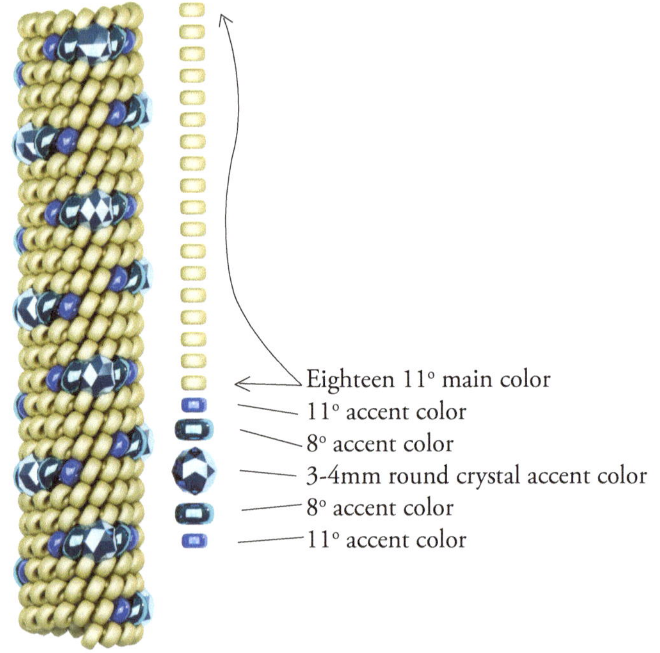

There is no law that says you must bead every stitch in your design, nor any that requires all beads to be the same size.

A beautiful fiber can speak quite nicely for itself. In this piece the fiber is 8/2 variegated tencel crocheted with a size 9 steel (1.25mm) crochet hook. The beads range in graduating size from 11° to 4mm.

The number of unbeaded rounds decreases toward the fully beaded area, then increases again.

Bead sizes (small to large)

Japanese 11°

Preciosa 9°

Matsuno 8°

Preciosa 6°

4mm round crystal

As your bead size increases, work rounds alternating beads of the sizes on either side. For example, the round of all 9° would be followed by one round alternating 9° and 8°, then one round of all 8°. This method of increasing sizes creates a smooth transition.

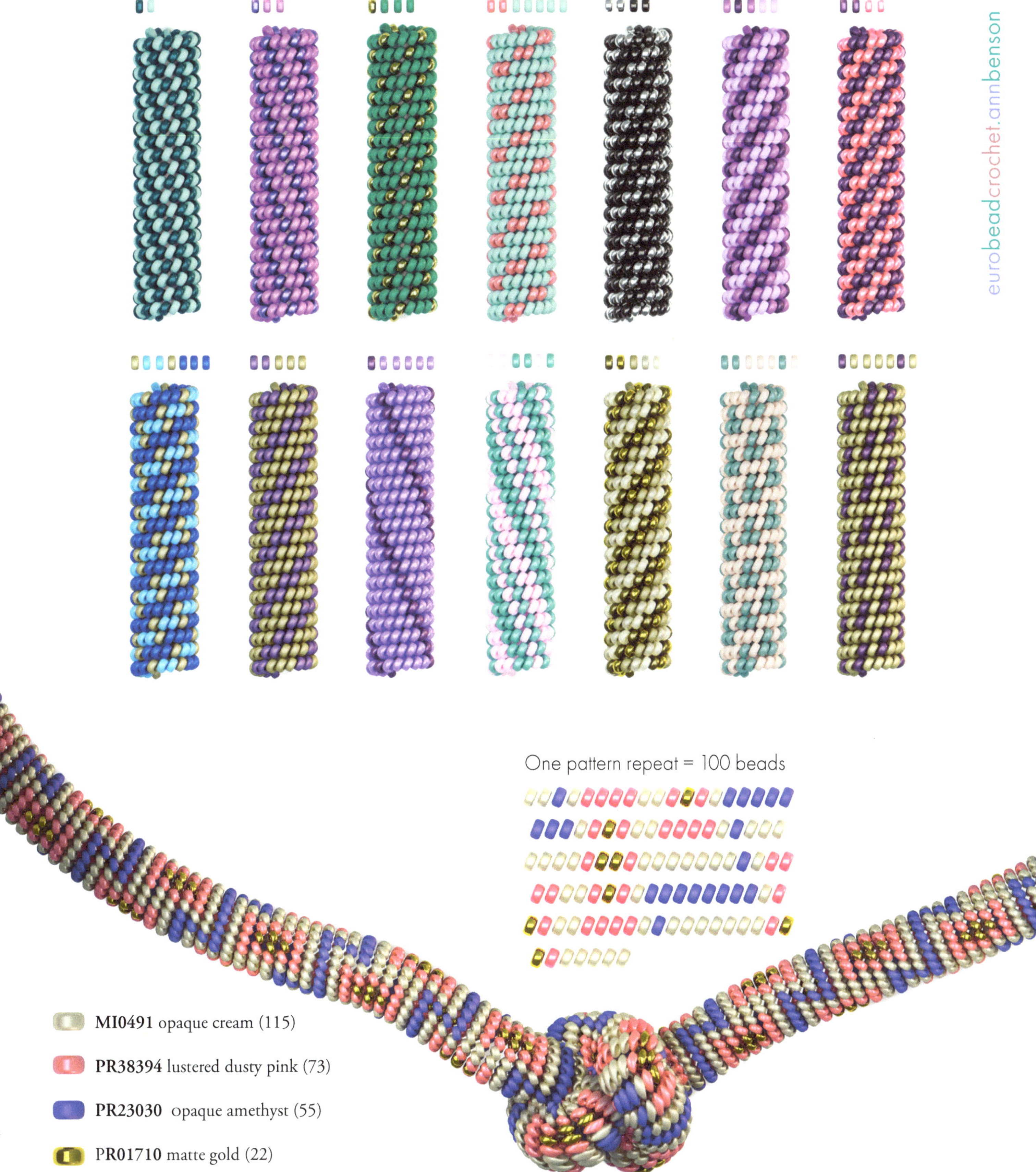

One pattern repeat = 100 beads

MI0491 opaque cream (115)

PR38394 lustered dusty pink (73)

PR23030 opaque amethyst (55)

PR01710 matte gold (22)

18-around patterns

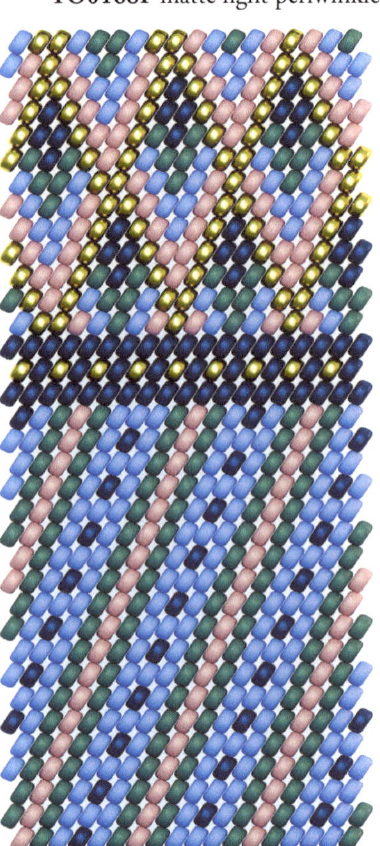

SECTION 1

- PR01710 matte light gold (171)
- TO0167BDF matte deep aqua AB (750)
- TO0764 matte bisque (480)
- PR33060M matte dark blue (295)
- TO0168F matte light periwinkle AB (675)

This design should be threaded from the chart, section 1 first, section 2 next, and section 3 last. As always with charted patterns, start at the top row of each section and add beads left to right, top row to bottom row. The first bead threaded will be the last bead stitched, so the first section threaded appears to be the bottom section. It's not! It will magically become the top as you crochet.

Each separately threaded section is joined to the previous section . The crochet continues seamlessly, creating a unified tube with no visible joints.

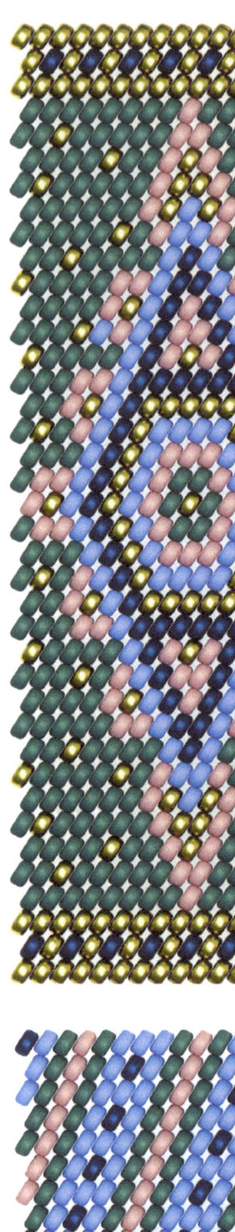

SECTION 2

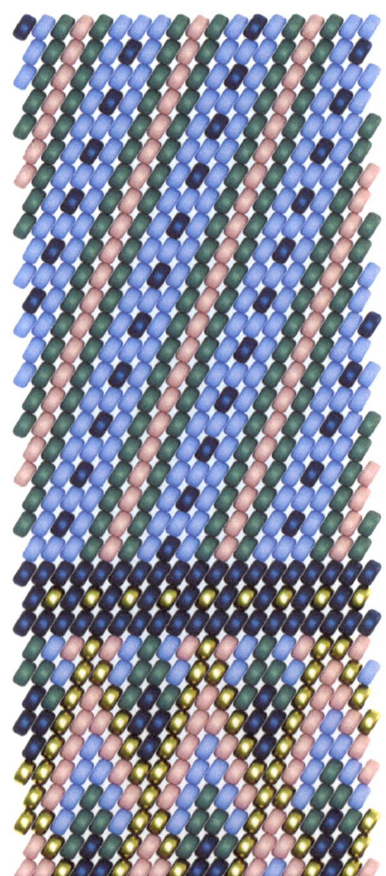

SECTION 3

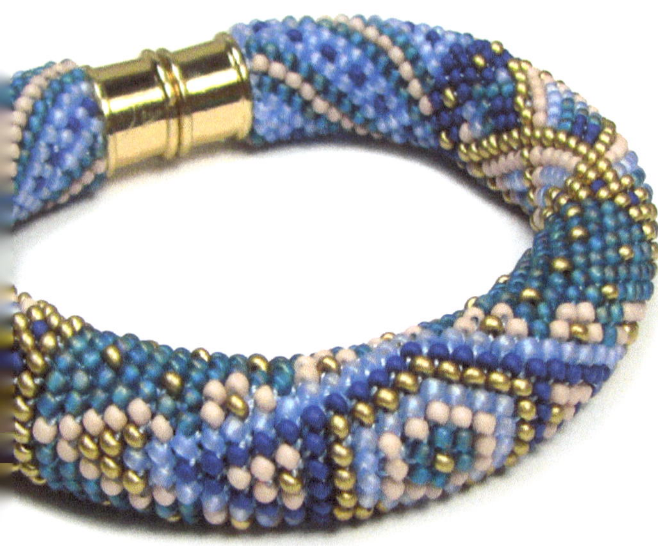

Design blank 18-around

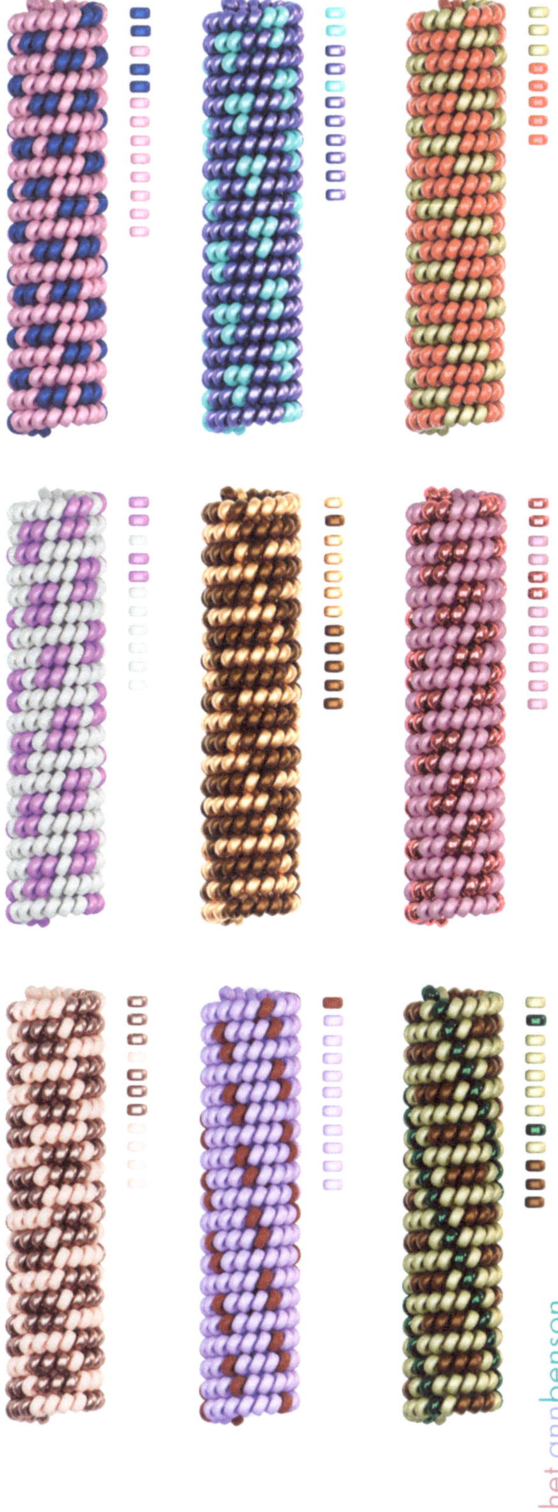

18-around patterns

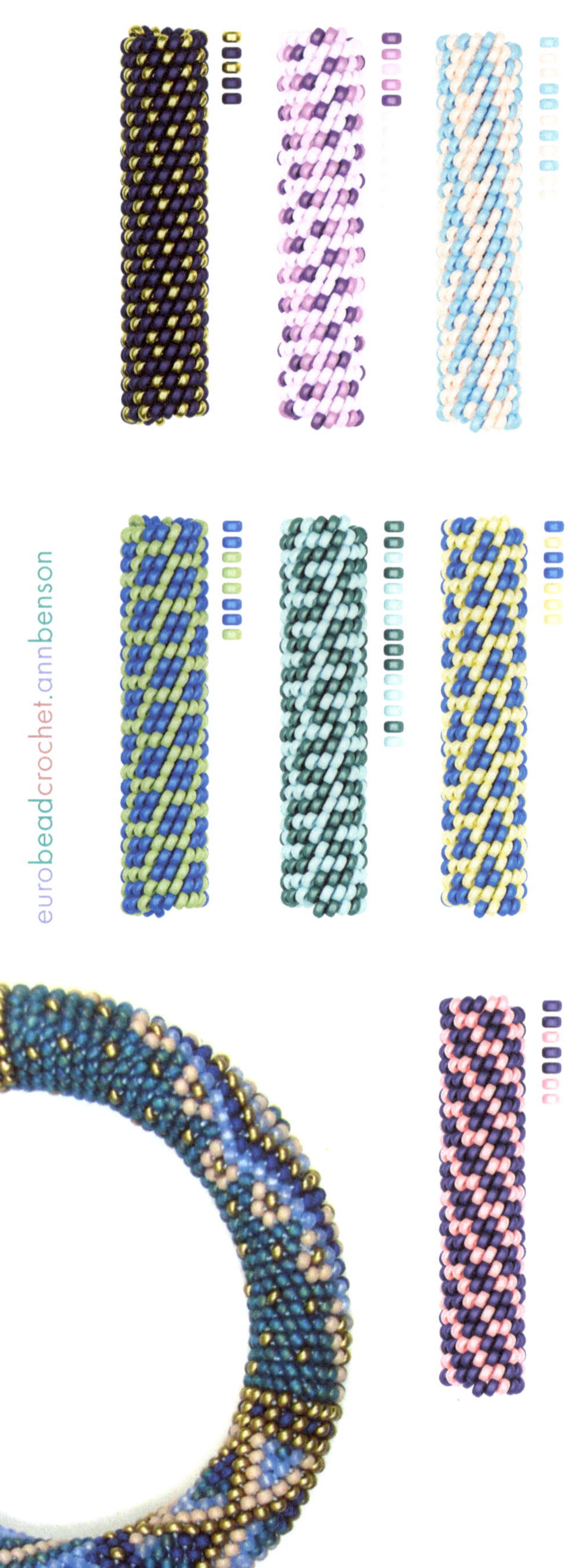

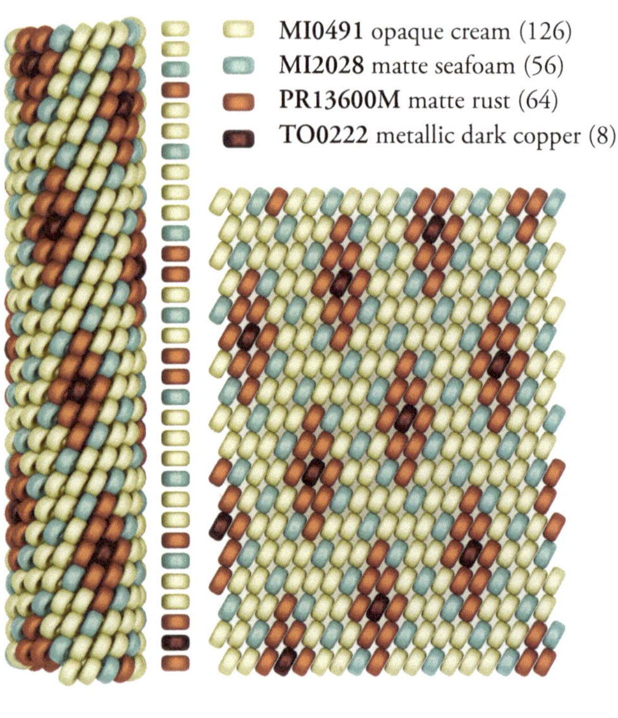

- ▢ **MI0491** opaque cream (126)
- ▢ **MI2028** matte seafoam (56)
- ▢ **PR13600M** matte rust (64)
- ▢ **TO0222** metallic dark copper (8)

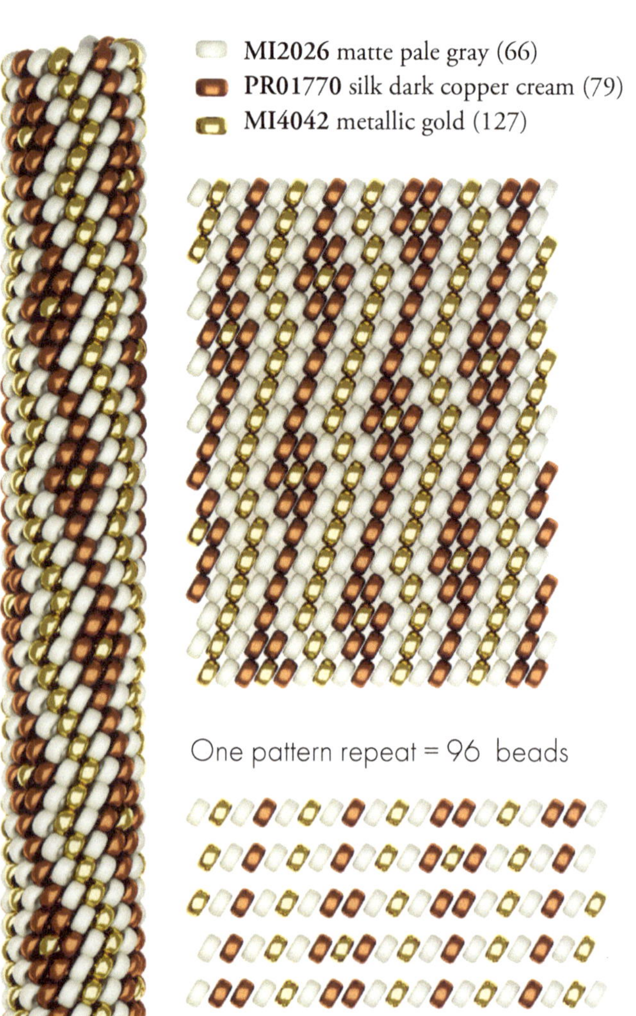

- ▢ **MI2026** matte pale gray (66)
- ▢ **PR01770** silk dark copper cream (79)
- ▢ **MI4042** metallic gold (127)

One pattern repeat = 96 beads

44

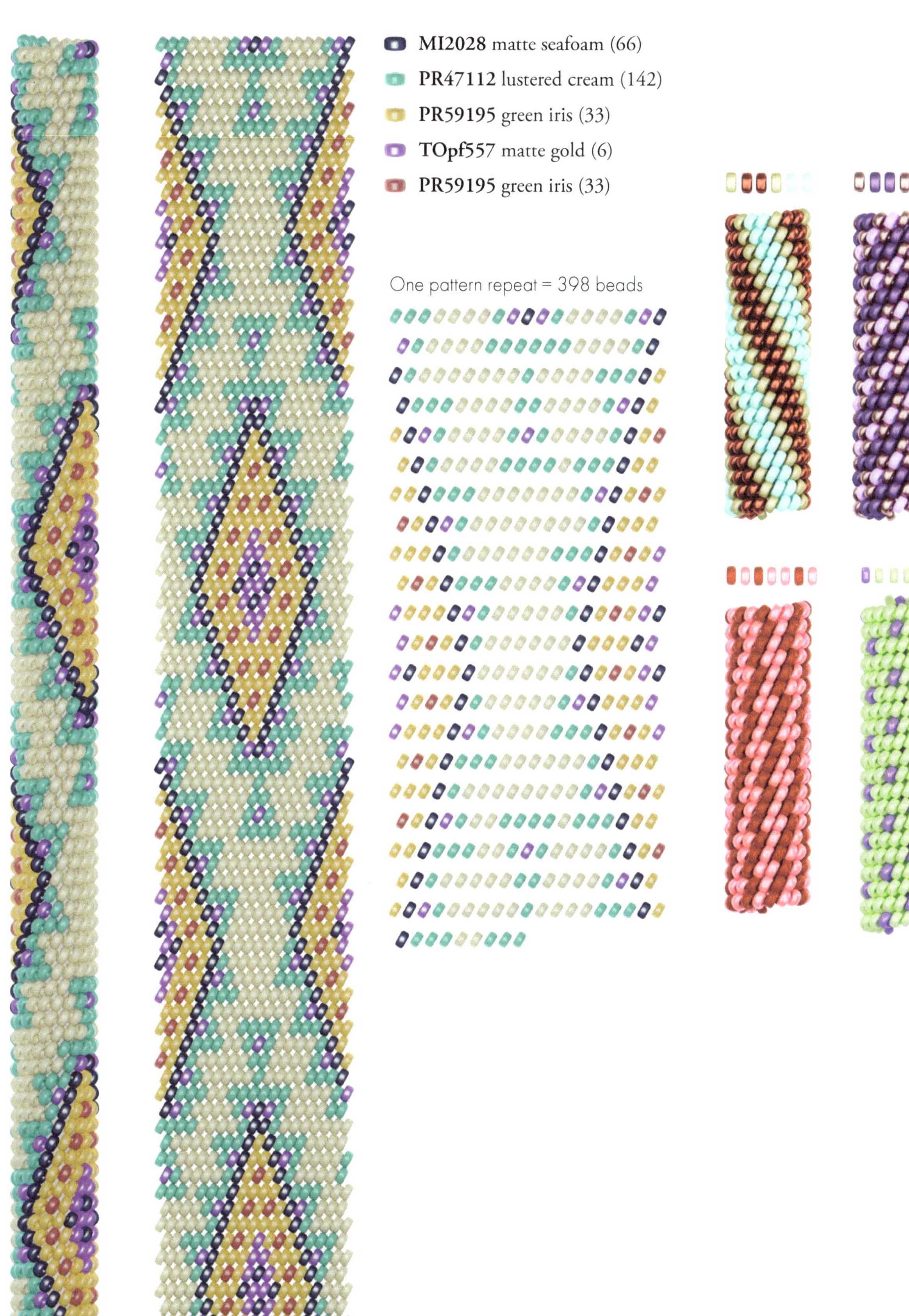

- **MI2028** matte seafoam (66)
- **PR47112** lustered cream (142)
- **PR59195** green iris (33)
- **TOpf557** matte gold (6)
- **PR59195** green iris (33)

One pattern repeat = 398 beads

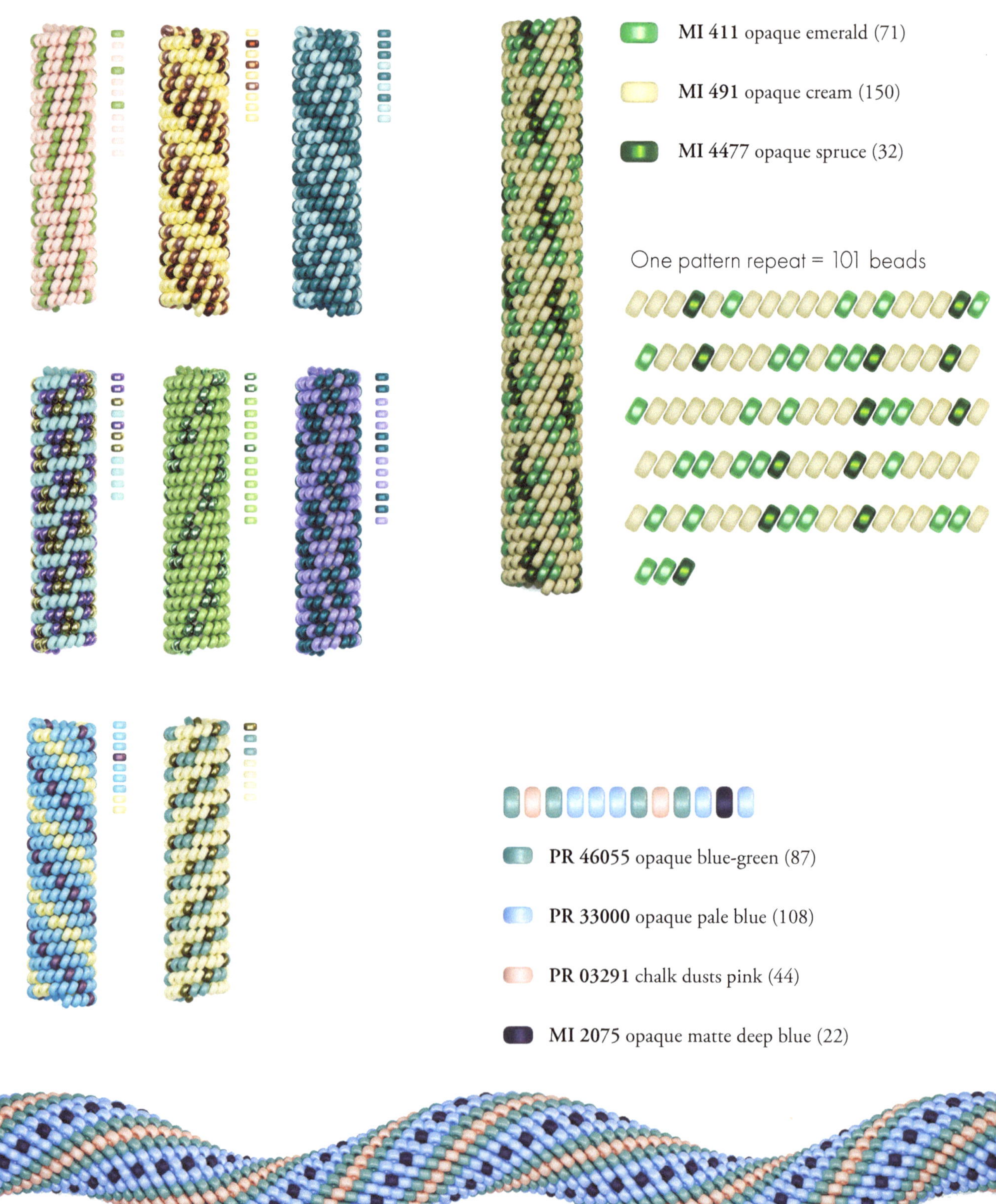

MI 411 opaque emerald (71)

MI 491 opaque cream (150)

MI 4477 opaque spruce (32)

One pattern repeat = 101 beads

PR 46055 opaque blue-green (87)

PR 33000 opaque pale blue (108)

PR 03291 chalk dusts pink (44)

MI 2075 opaque matte deep blue (22)

19-around patterns

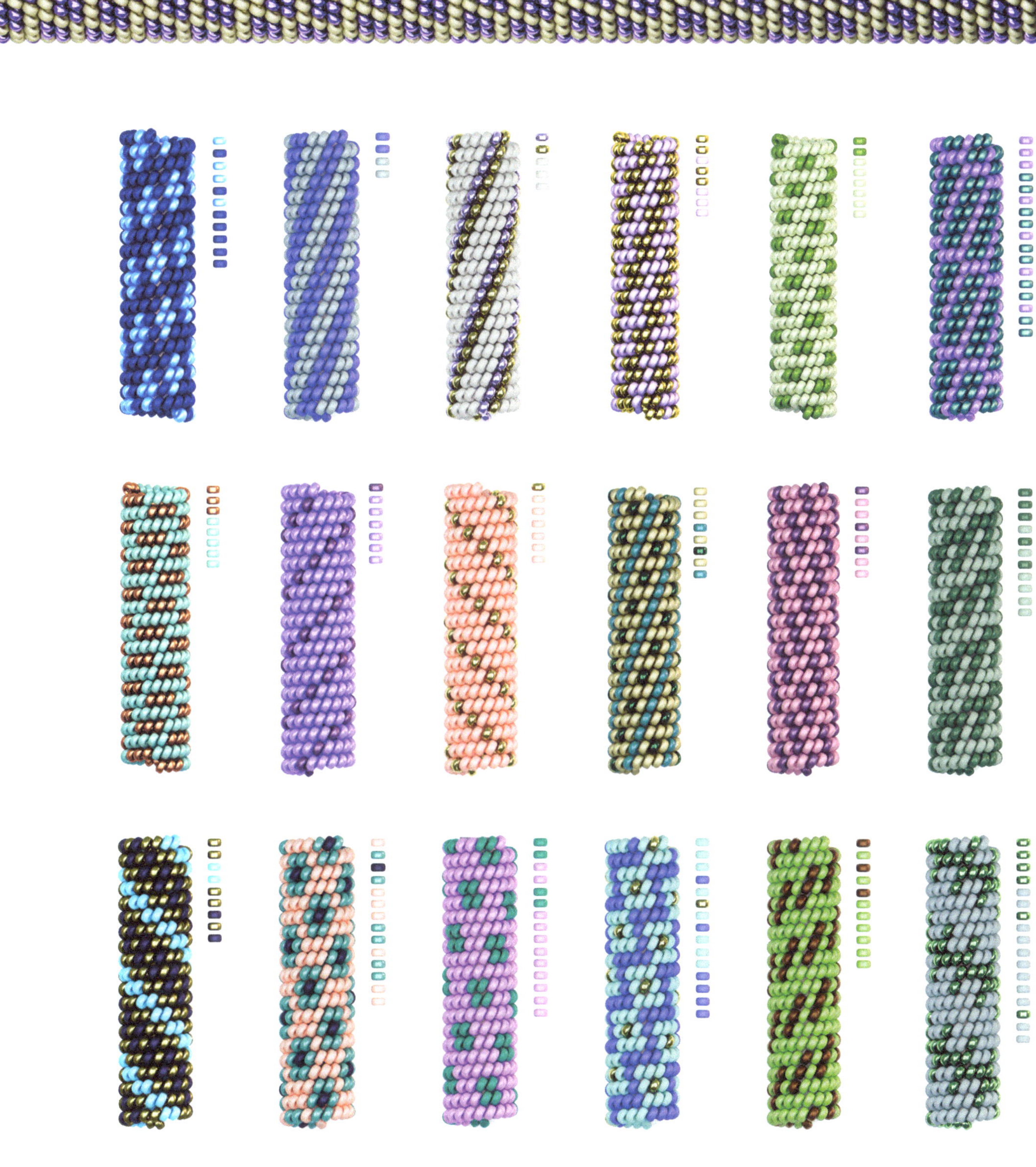

19-around patterns
Red Paisley

PR93170 opaque red (129)

MI4202 duracoat gold (45)

PR07331 chalk light rose (57)

TO1634F matte amethyst AB (76)

MI2028 matte seafoam AB (43)

One pattern repeat = 312 beads

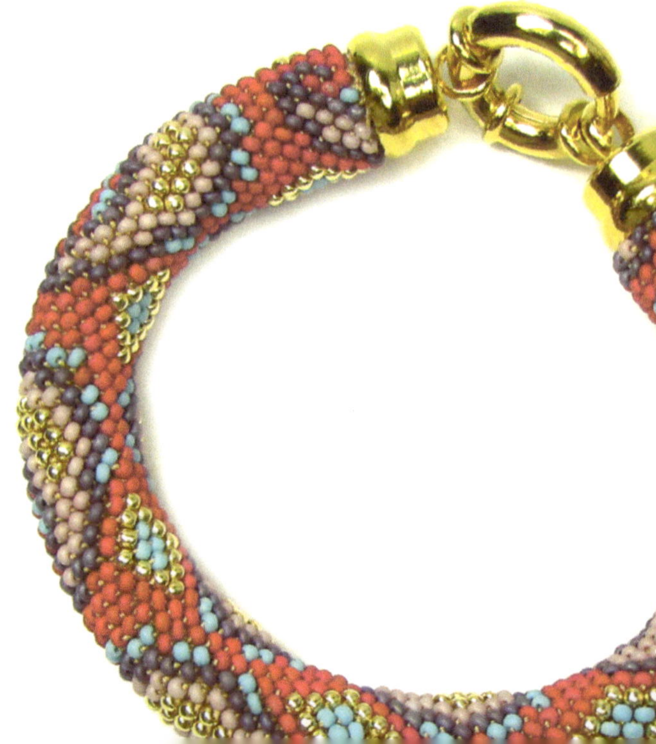

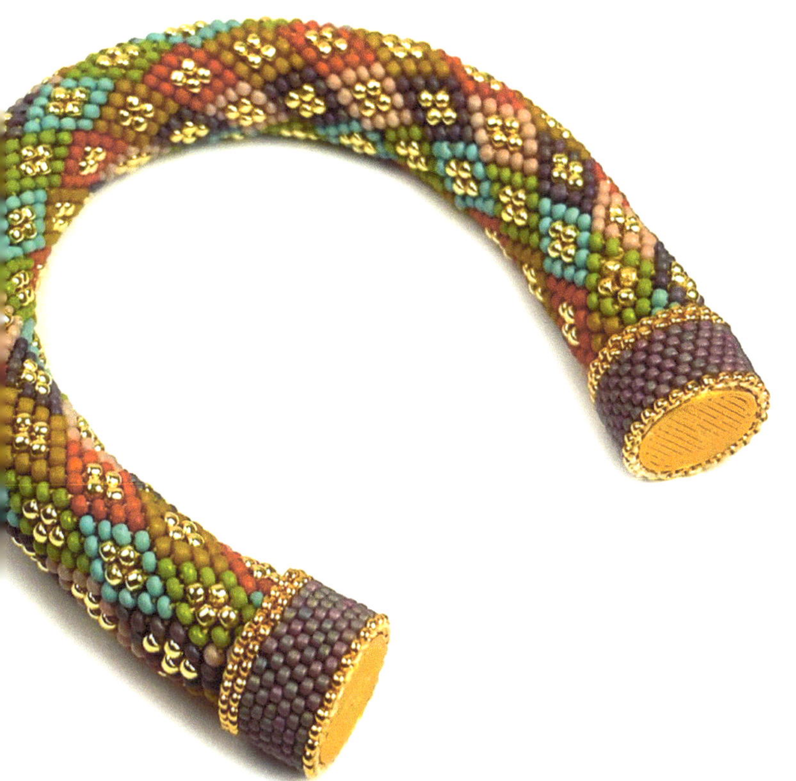

19-around patterns
Rainbow Argyle

- **MI4202** duracoat gold (62)
- **PR93170** opaque red (34)
- **MI4456** matte ochre (34)
- **TO 1634F** matte amethyst AB (34)
- **PR07331** chalk light rose (34)
- **PR63130** opaque turquoise (34)
- **PR53430** opaque olive AB (34)

One pattern repeat = 192 beads

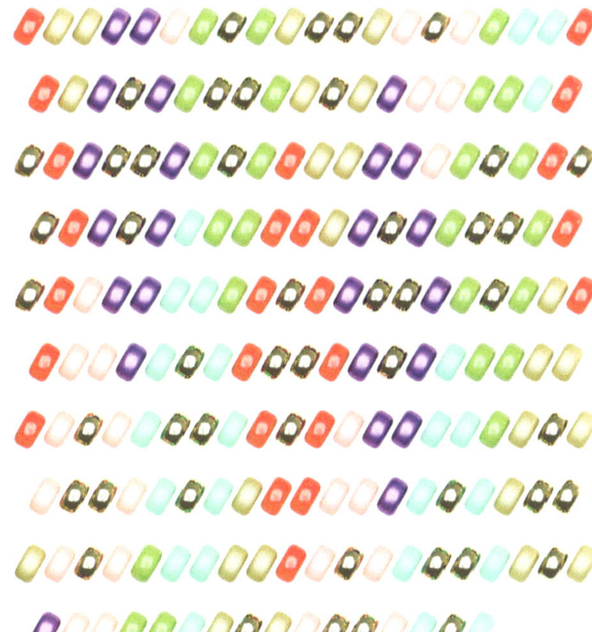

19-around patterns

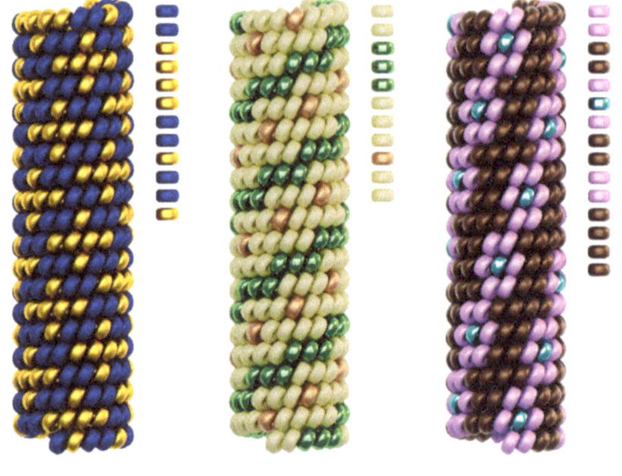

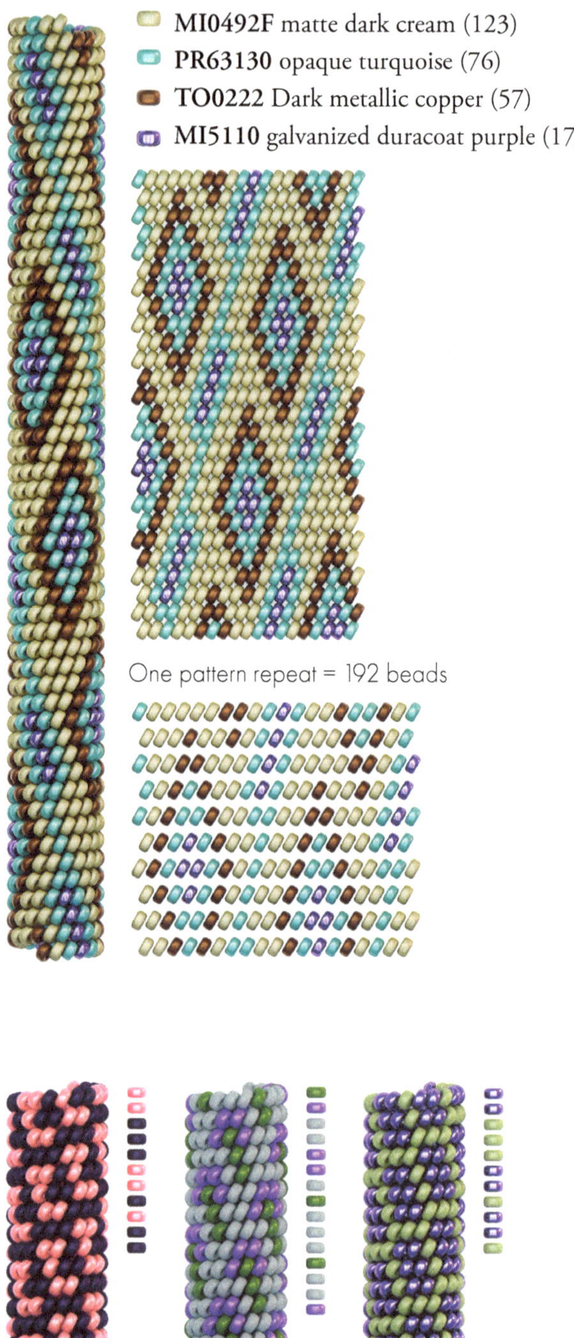

MI0492F matte dark cream (123)
PR63130 opaque turquoise (76)
TO0222 Dark metallic copper (57)
MI5110 galvanized duracoat purple (17)

One pattern repeat = 192 beads

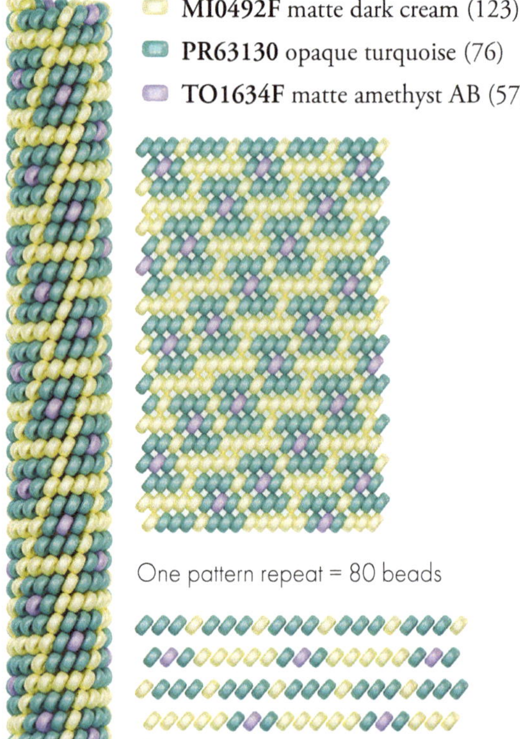

MI0492F matte dark cream (123)
PR63130 opaque turquoise (76)
TO1634F matte amethyst AB (57)

One pattern repeat = 80 beads

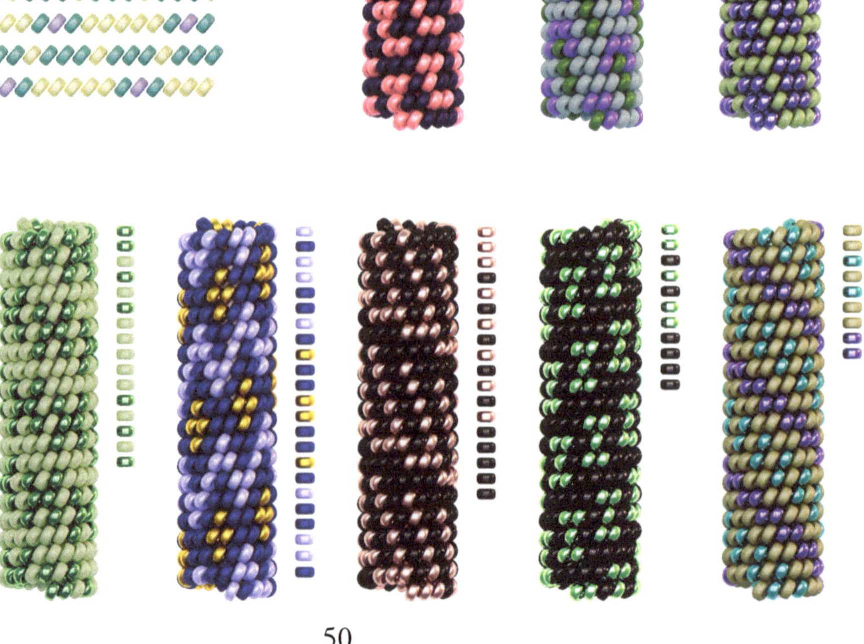

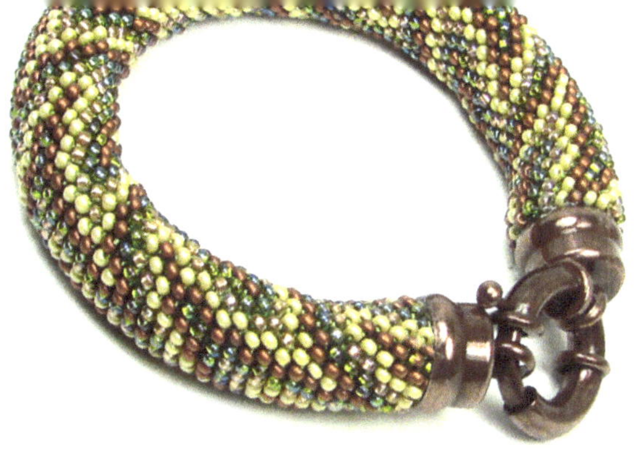

- **PR01750** silk dark copper (78)
- **PR59349** brass-lined emerald (72)
- **PR68505** copper-lined crystal (36)
- **PR47112** opaque beige (72)

One pattern repeat = 90 beads

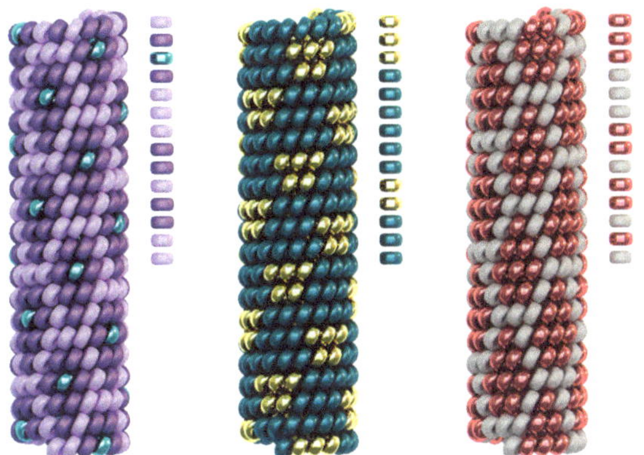

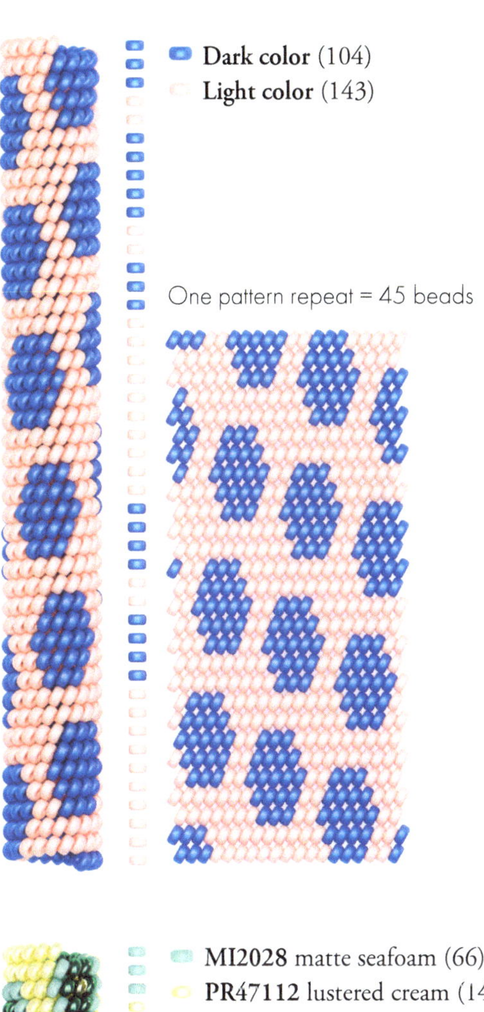

- **Dark color** (104)
- **Light color** (143)

One pattern repeat = 45 beads

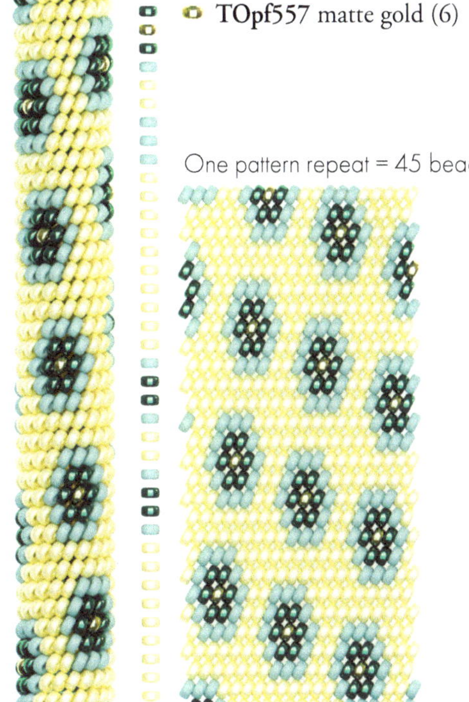

- **MI2028** matte seafoam (66)
- **PR47112** lustered cream (142)
- **PR59195** green iris (33)
- **TOpf557** matte gold (6)

One pattern repeat = 45 beads

Design blank 19-around

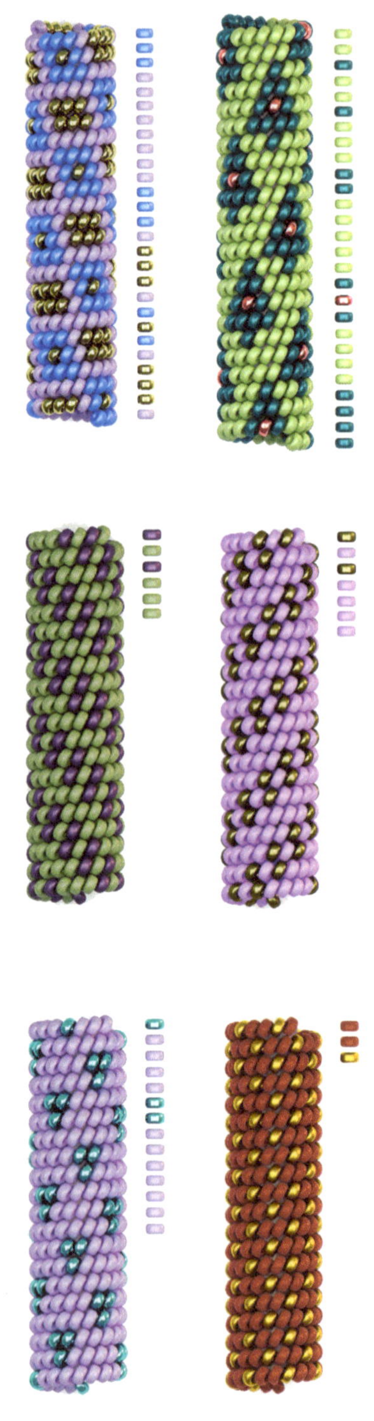

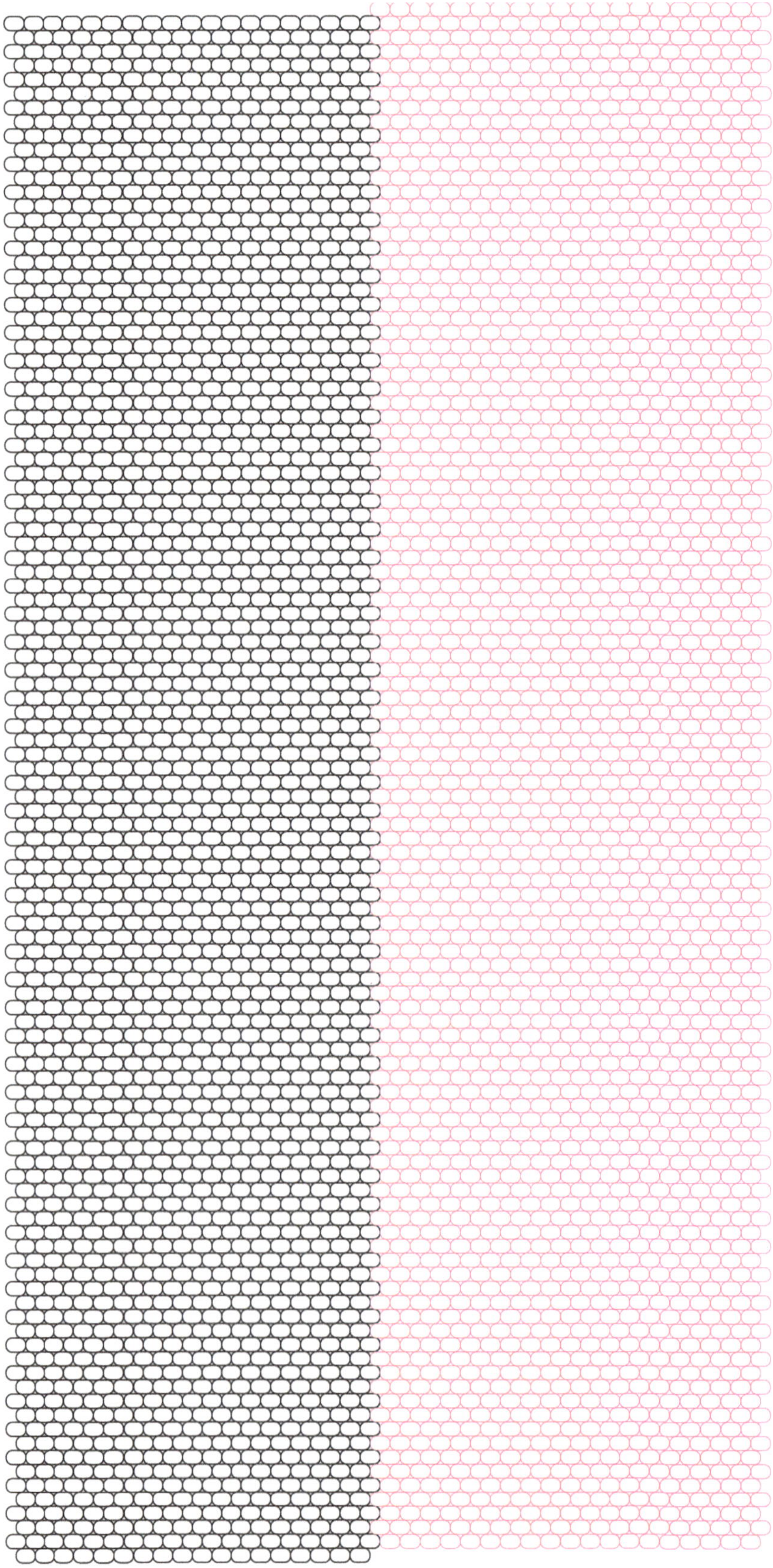

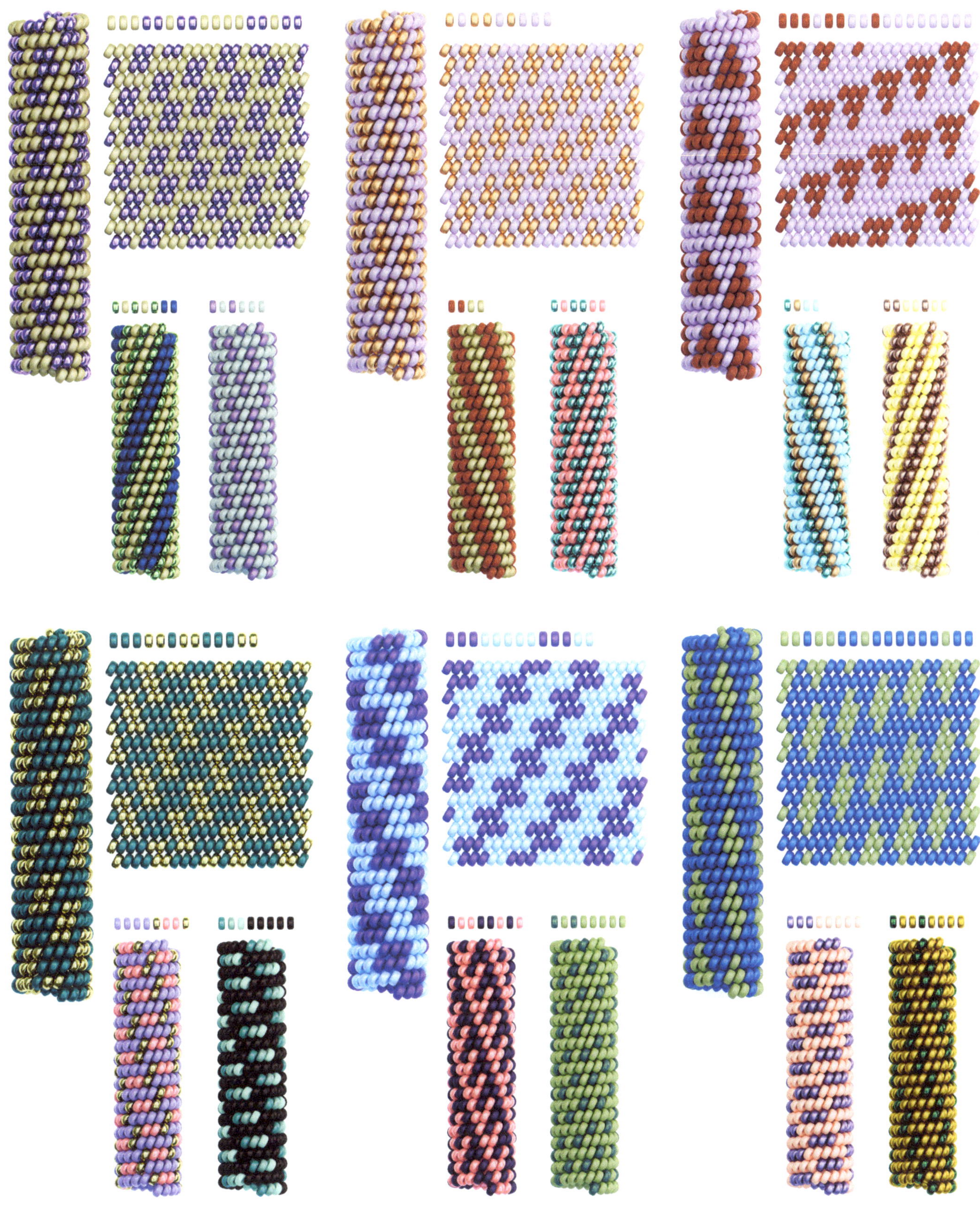

20-around patterns

Design blank 20-around

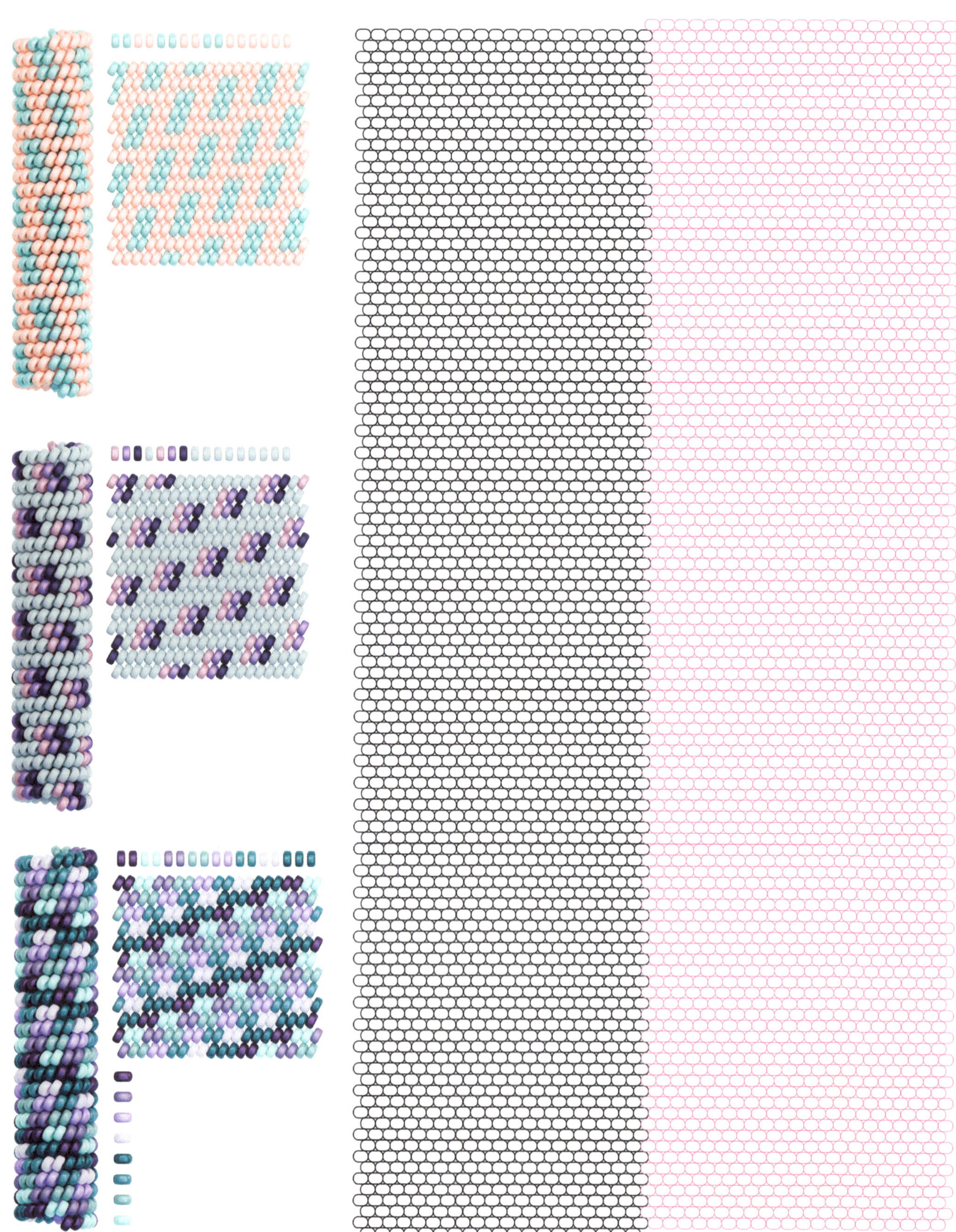

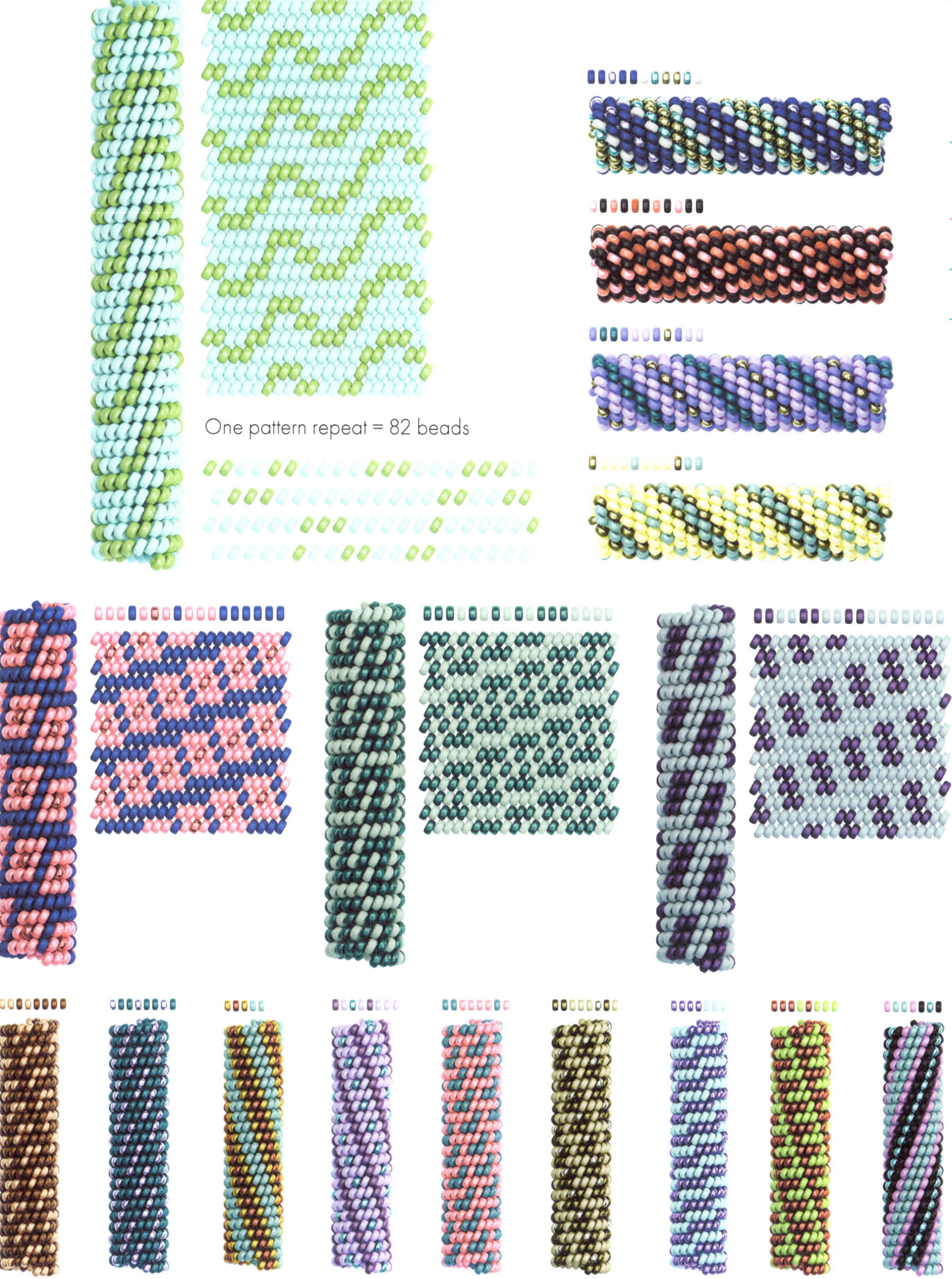

One pattern repeat = 82 beads

20-around patterns

The length of the tube threaded as shown will be about 7" when stitched fully in 11°s. For a longer tube, try using 10°s or even 9°s which will yield greater length.

MATERIAL AMOUNTS ARE FOR THE ENTIRE PATTERN

- MI0491 opaque cream (589)
- MI4456 matte ochre (382)
- **PR13600M matte** light rust (518)
- MI4492 duracoat brown (205)
- MI0401 opaque jet black (582))

SECTION 1

SECTION 3

combining multiple tubes

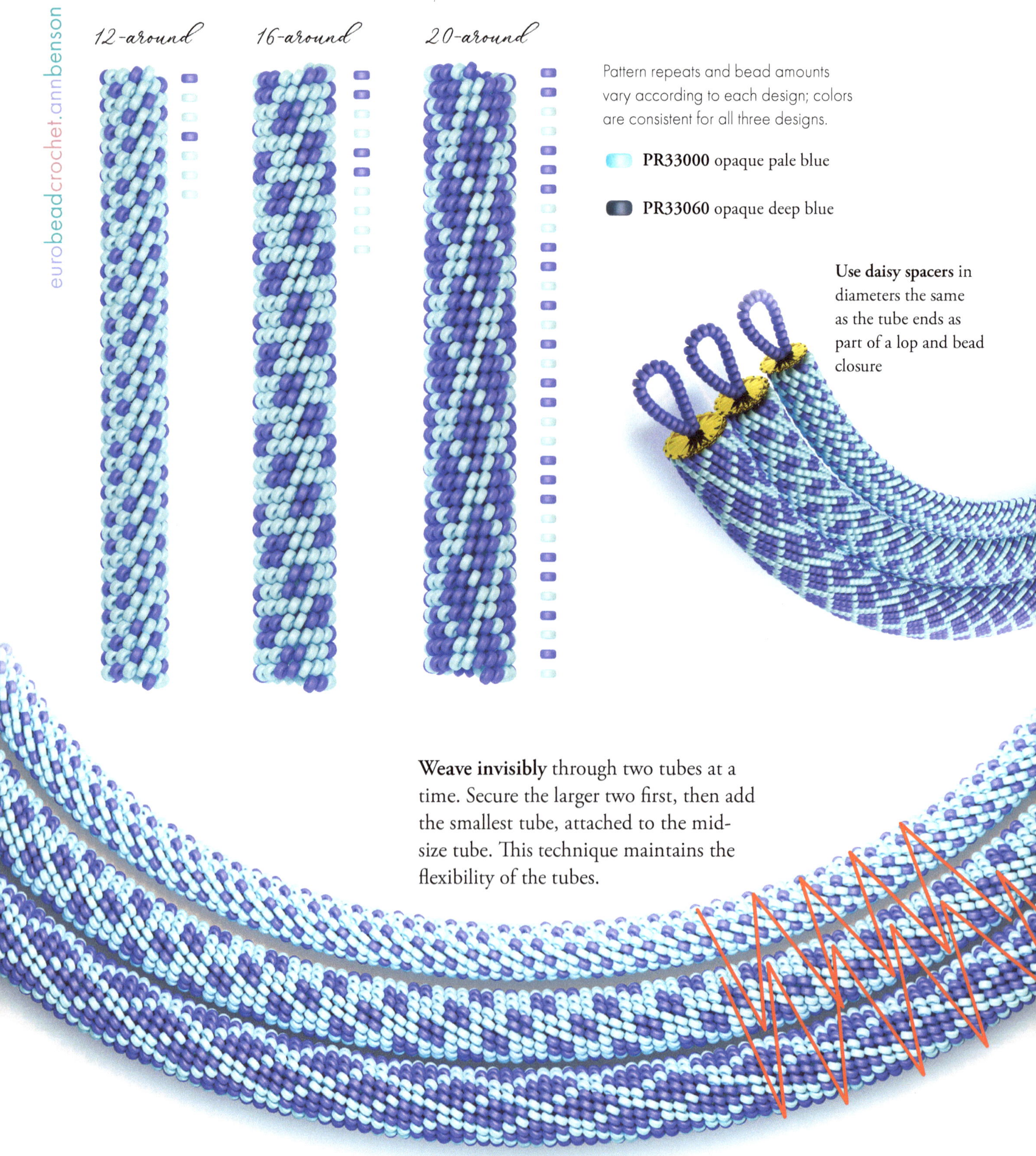

12-around   16-around   20-around

Pattern repeats and bead amounts vary according to each design; colors are consistent for all three designs.

PR33000 opaque pale blue

PR33060 opaque deep blue

Use daisy spacers in diameters the same as the tube ends as part of a lop and bead closure

Weave invisibly through two tubes at a time. Secure the larger two first, then add the smallest tube, attached to the mid-size tube. This technique maintains the flexibility of the tubes.

Your finished tube needs core support.

My favorite method is to use a bundle of leftover scrap fibers. You can also use rubber tubing of the appropriate diameter for the channel of your tube, but the correct diameter may be difficult to find. Cut a length of grouped fibers a bit longer than twice the length of your tube. Fold it in half and use a hooked wire (about 2" longer than the tube) to pull it through the tube's open core. Using a supporting bundle of fibers—pulled through the tube with wire—solves the diameter issue and maintains tube flexibility. You can add or remove individual fibers until the diameter is precisely correct, and the tube has a good appearance.

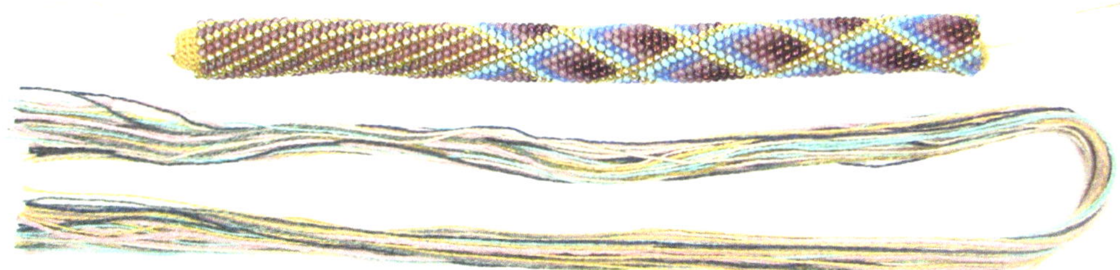

Cotton, wool, light linen, and synthetics will work nicely. Fold the bundle in half. Cut a scrap or light wire (24-gauge or thinner) about two inches longer than your tube.

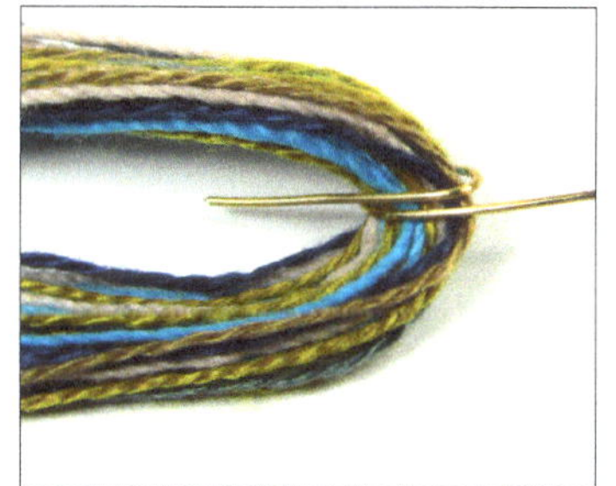

Fold the fiber bundle in half and loop the wire end around it so the cut end of the wire is facing away from the rest of the wire. This will prevent snagging as you pull the fibers through the tube.

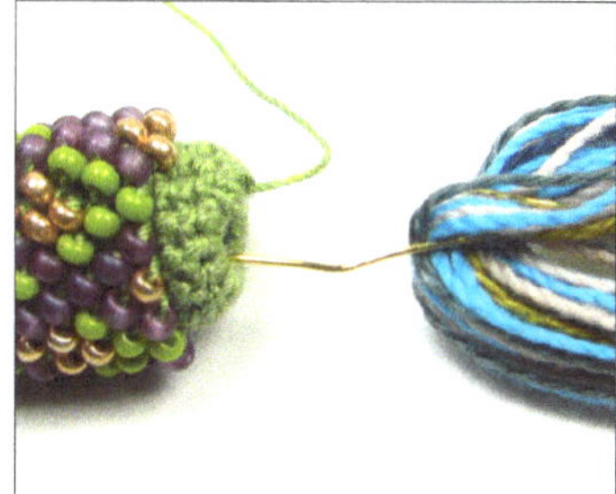

Straighten the wire and run-rotate it through the channel. Start with all the fiber strands; if the bulk is too much, pull the bundle back out and remove fiber strands as needed for a good fit.

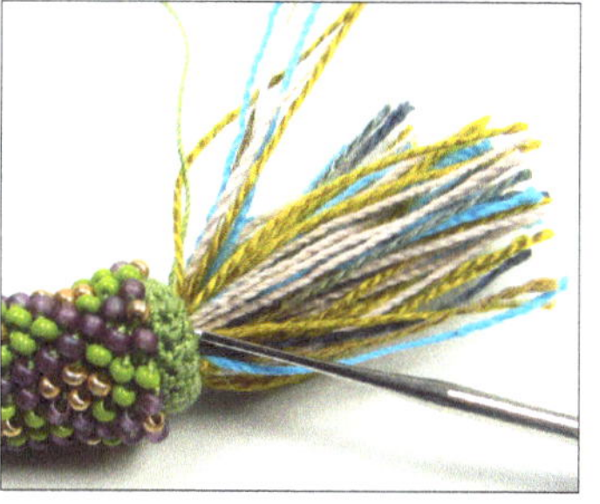

Use the hook to pull out the un-beaded rounds if they are drawn into the tube with the fibers.

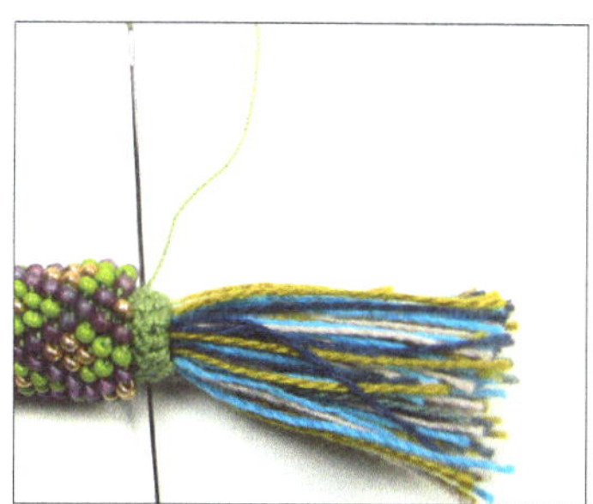

When you're satisfied with the fill, use the thread tails on both ends to roughly secure the fiber bundle. Make several passes back and forth. Don't cut the crochet tails if they will be needed in your finishing method.

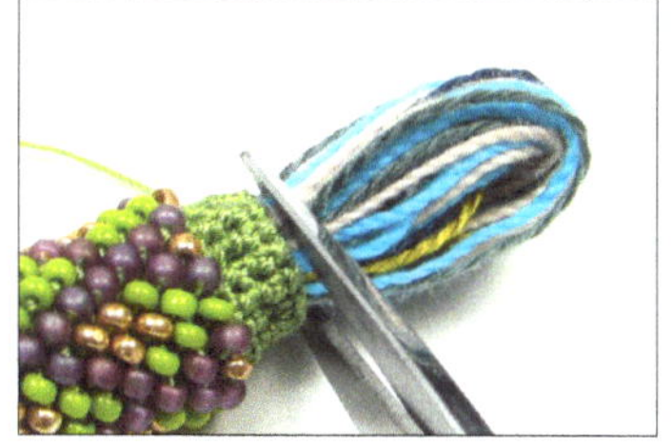

Trim the secured fibers at both ends of the crochet. Take care not to cut the crochet stitches.

The example shown here features a short section crocheted without beads for a specific kind of cap, but a fiber core is also effective for designs where the beads are added in the first round. In that case, secure the fibers within the initial chain round and dab the end with flexible fabric glue to secure the cut ends of the support fiber.

Adding a closure to your project

A clasp, button, snap, or seamless joint can bring your beautiful crocheted tube to an absolutely gorgeous finish.

Use the best quality closure you can afford; some inexpensive closures may lose their finish over time, or even worse, oxidize (rust!). When using fully-metal clasps, go for quality—gold-filled or sterling silver, unlikely to wear—if they're in your budget. If not, try a beaded clasp (you can make these yourself), a button and loop, a good quality snap, or—depending on the nature of your design—a fun plastic closure. Polymer clay bead caps are a great idea.

Using a spring clasp with a bar

Shown with cap adjacent to the beads; requires three unbeaded rounds at both ends. You can also insert the beaded end INTO the cap; requires only one unbeaded round at both ends.

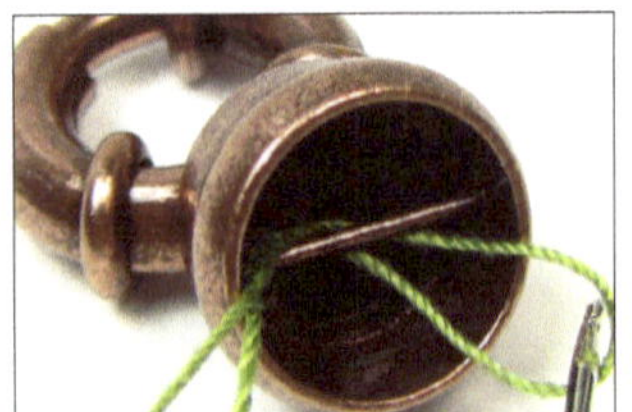 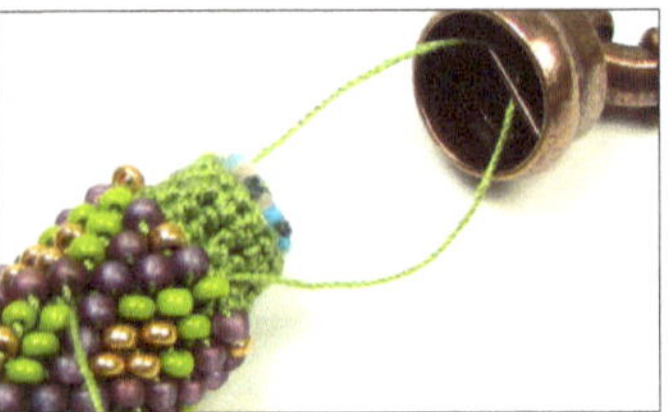 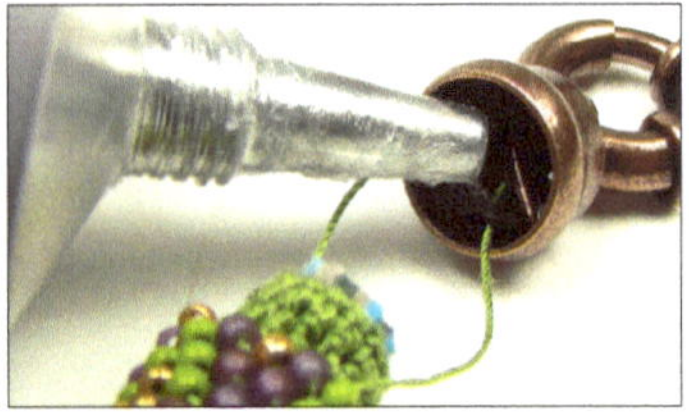 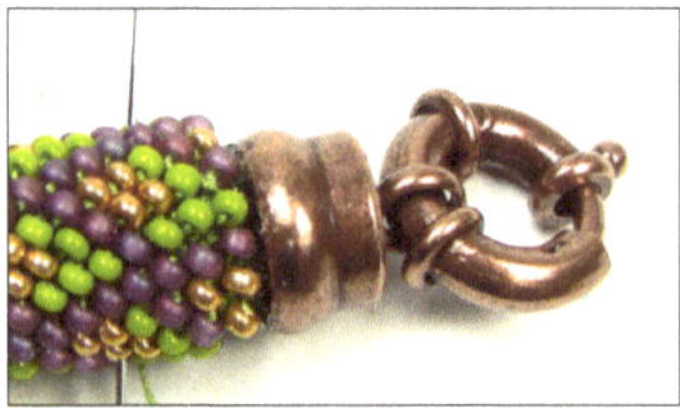

Fold the thread tail to form a loop and push the loop into the clasp end so it emerges beyond the bar. Use your hook to pull the tail out.	Run the thread through the unbeaded rounds and down into the tube so it emerges from the side of the beaded area. Do not run through bead holes.	Half-fill the clasp end with glue and pull the thread so the clasp end covers the unbeaded rounds and cut fibers. Some glue SHOULD ooze out and touch the beads of the outer round.	Secure the thread tail within the tube by running it back and forth a few times. It's okay to run through the center of the tub now. Trim the tail thread so it disappears into the tube.

Simple magnetic clasps

What could be easier? Your clasp should have the same inside diameter as your tube or unbeaded end. Make sure the magnets are strong. I highly recommend using a safety chain or strand of beads if you're nervous about the strength of your clasp.

A safety strap (beads or chain) can be added from one end to the other for security. When worn, most of the strap will disappear behind the bracelet

Seamless end joint

Unlike slip-stitch bead crochet, Euro crochet does not lend itself easily to an invisible join. The starting and ending chains always will be visible.

That said, you can join one end of a tube to another for a roll-on bracelet AFTER adding/trimming the support fibers. Stitch the ends together as neatly as possible with strong sewing thread or nylon beading thread. Then wrap a strip of leather or a band of peyote stitch around the joint to cover it.

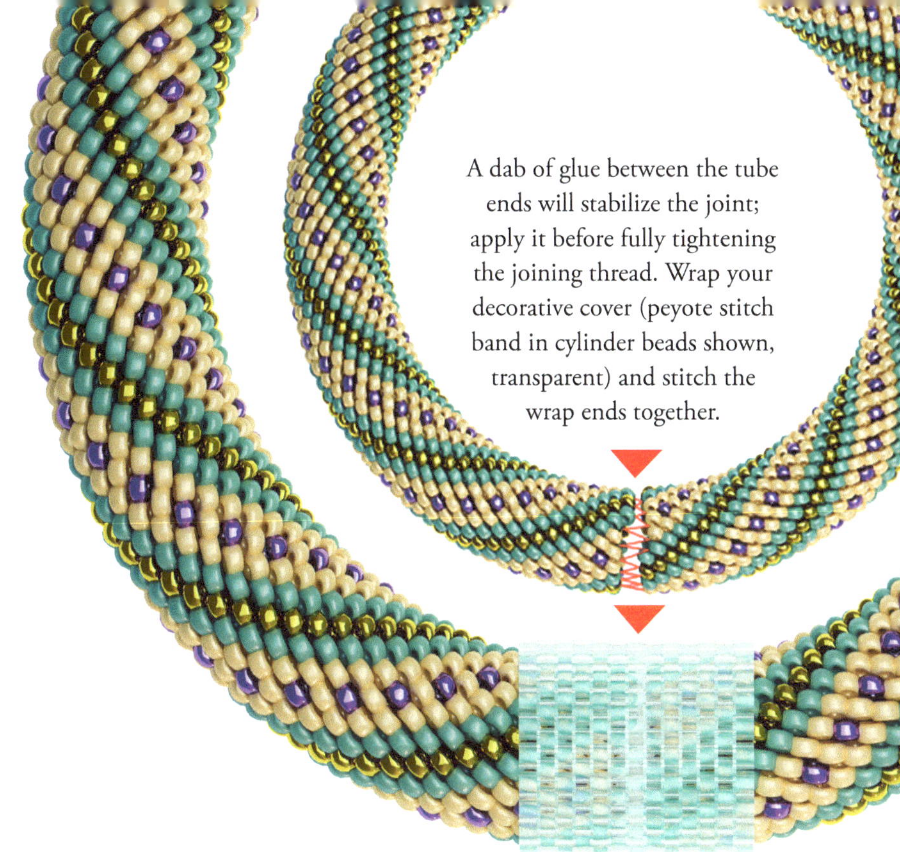

A dab of glue between the tube ends will stabilize the joint; apply it before fully tightening the joining thread. Wrap your decorative cover (peyote stitch band in cylinder beads shown, transparent) and stitch the wrap ends together.

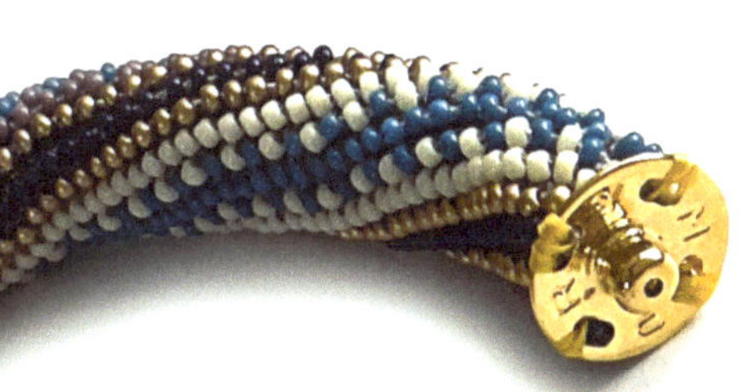

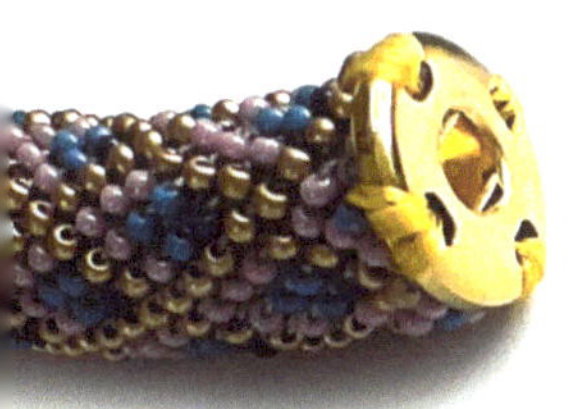

Snap closure

A snap closure, while it can be difficult to put on your wrist without assistance, is comfortable to wear and discreet. Use strong sewing thread or nylon beading thread in a color that closely approximates the color of your snap. Snaps are available in a wide variety of diameters, as well as in silver, gold and black. Dab glue on the ends of your core thread bundle before sewing the snap in place.

Button and loop closure

Use beautiful bead caps with the same inside diameter as your tube's outside diameter. Caps should be glued in place for stability; you will be sacrificing a needle in this process as it will be passed through glue.

Before adding the glue, bring a doubled thread (size D beading nylon) out of the end of the supported tube. You can knot the end to secure it. Run through the hole in the cap, then dab glue on the tube end around the thread's emergence point. Pick up three or four 11°s and your button, then add whatever anchoring beads will hold the button in place. Run back through the cap's hole and into the tube end. If you can manage it, make a second pass through the button for strength. You can bring the thread out of the side of the tube below the cap; run back and forth lightly through the tube to secure the thread. Trim carefully.

To create the loop on the opposite end, bring out the doubled thread and add just enough beads to fit over the button. Run back through the cap hole, and complete as you did for the button end.

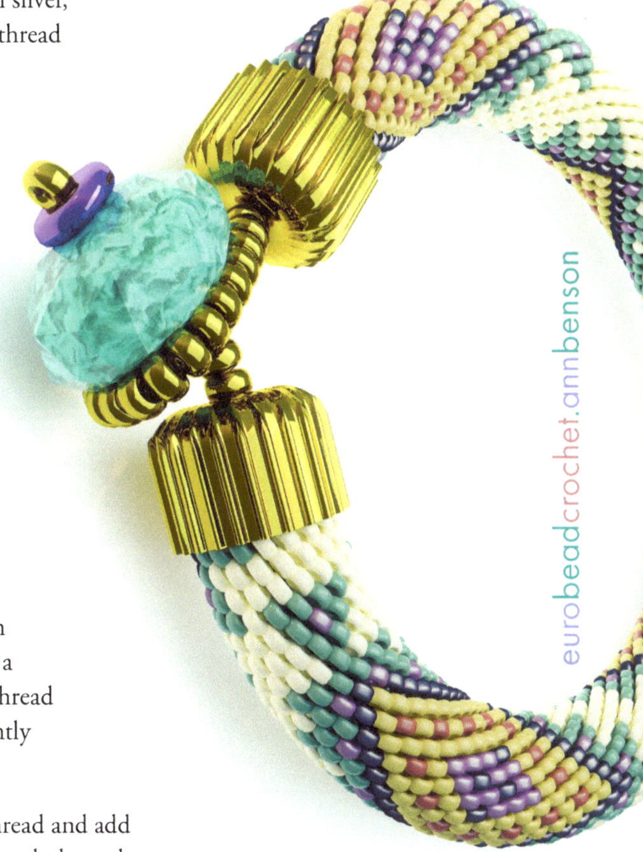

Design blank 12-around

Design blank 14-around

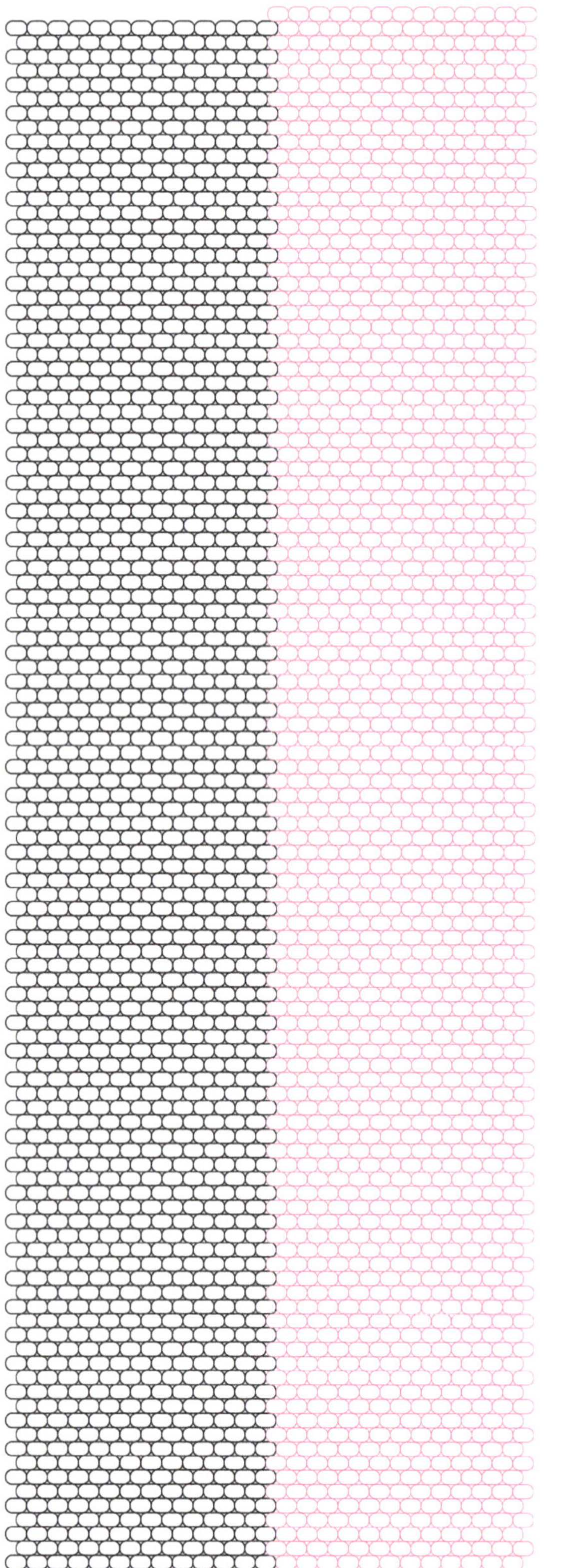

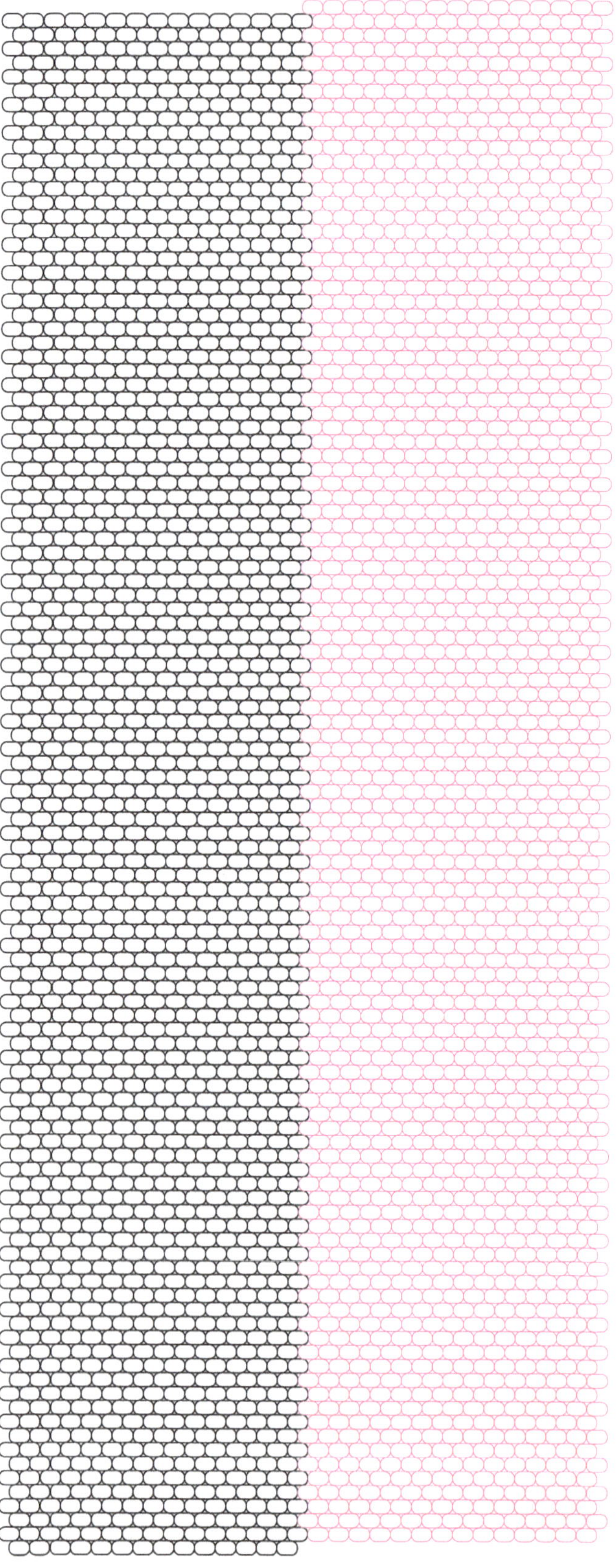

Design blank 16-around

Design blank 18-around

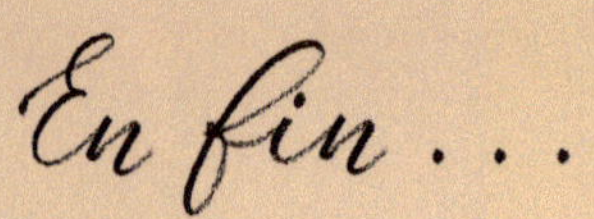

Care and Feeding

With minimal care your creation will last decades.

Avoid **excess surface wear** and handling to keep your beads shiny and brilliant.

Avoid getting **cosmetics** such as moisturizers on the beads.

A dampened cloth rubbed LIGHTLY on the surface of your beads will often suffice to freshen the appearance as glass is largely impermeable and dirt will be on the surface.

Avoid getting the crochet thread and core support thread wet.

If you use a loop closure with a beading or sewing thread core, **replace the threading from time to time** as thin thread may wear over time.

Permissions

You may use any of the patterns in this publication in your personal crafting without restriction.

You may reprint sections of this publication to facilitate personal crafting in order to preserve the original material for reuse. Reprinted patterns may not be sold or given away.

You may create and thereafter sell an item created from a pattern in this publication **with a legible design attribution** to the author, such as (in a small font): "Stitched by Mary Poppins, design by Ann Benson."

Teachers may use the general instruction material to teach others with prior written notification to and consent from the author, who can be contacted at annbensonbeading.com.

Software/hardware/fonts used in creating this book

Illustrations were created in Cinema4D (Maxon One) animation suite and Adobe Illustrator.

Photos and illustrations were processed in Adobe PhotoShop.

Layout and text were created in Adobe InDesign.

PDFs were developed in Adobe Acrobat.

Files (over 1000 illustrations, text blocks and graphics) were organized in Adobe Bridge and Apple Finder.

Photos were taken with iPhone 11, iPad Pro, and iPad mini.

Fonts are Garamond Pro (serif), Futura PT (sans serif) and Palomino (script).

The computer on which this was all completed is a MacBook Pro.

Sourcing

As of this writing, there are abundant sources for beads and threads on the internet.

I maintain a list of preferred sources on my site **annbensonbeading.com.** Go to the "sourcing" page to see links to vendors for beads, threads, finishing materials and more. As suppliers change regularly, this will be the most current offering of places to find what you need.

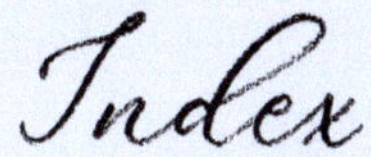

Index

Also from **Ann Benson:**

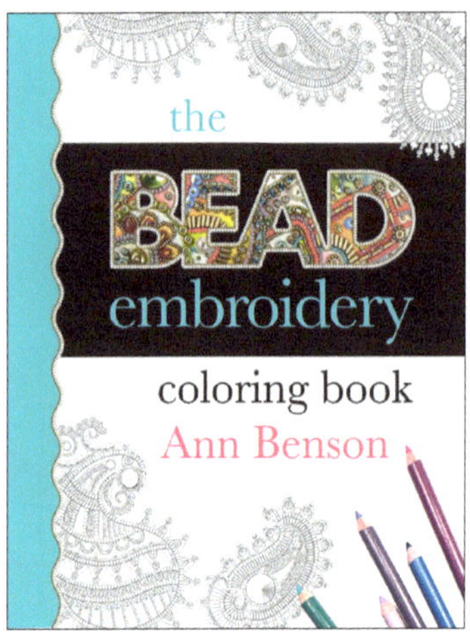

Paperback on Amazon
Digital Download on Etsy

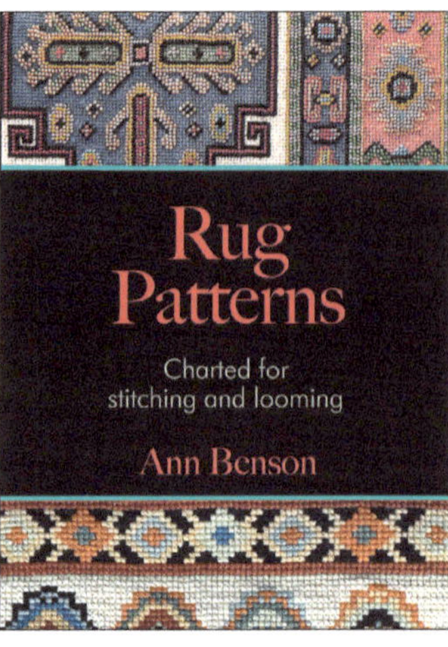

Paperback on Amazon
Digital Download on Etsy

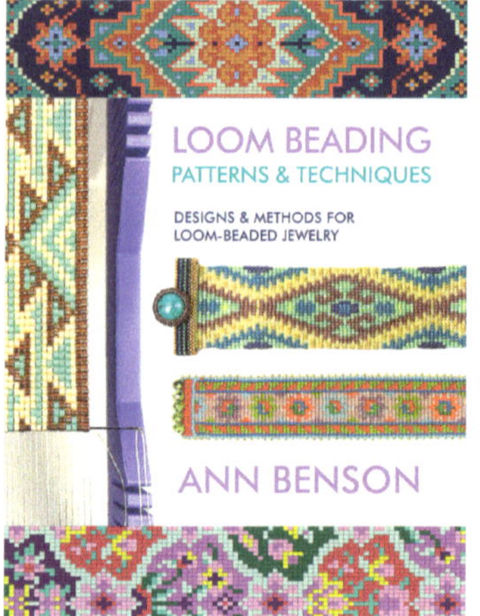

Paperback on Amazon
Digital Download on Etsy

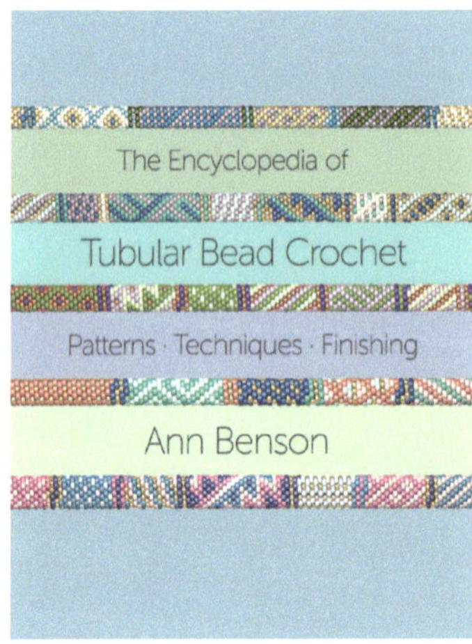

Paperback on Amazon
Digital Download on Etsy

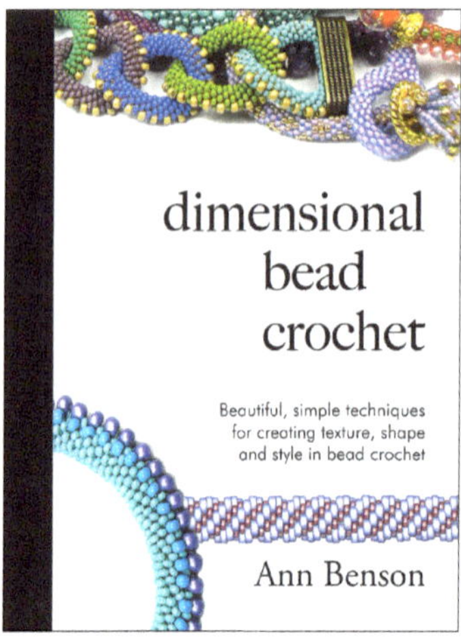

Paperback on Amazon
Digital Download on Etsy

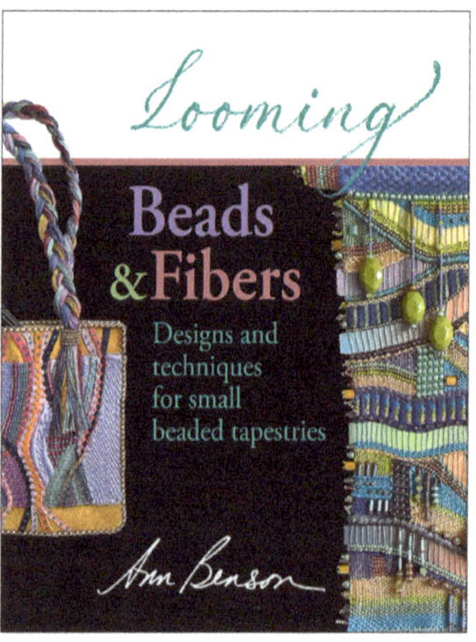

COMING SOON:
Paperback on Amazon
Digital Download on Etsy

About the author

Ann Benson is an American master bead and needle artist whose body of work includes hundreds of patterns, books and tutorials. She is a YouTube instructional influencer with millions of views and myriad followers. Ann holds a certification in graphic design from Rhode Island School of Design and is renowned for the clarity and thoroughness of her crafting instructions.

Ann is also the author of The Plague Trilogy historical novels (Random House) including *The Plague Tales, The Burning Road,* and *The Physician's Tale.* Ann's latest novel Ambrosia is published under her own imprint.

Ann divides her time between homes in Florida and Cape Cod, where she and husband Gary Frost enjoy their children, grandchildren and friends.

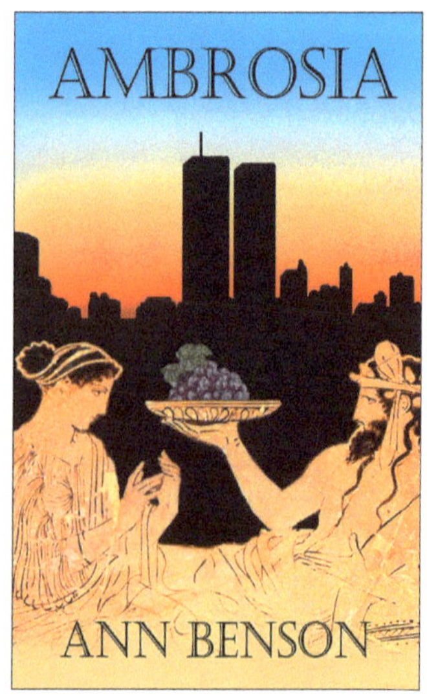